Simple Pottery

Simple Pottery
Kenneth Drake

Studio Vista

Watson-Guptill Publications   New York

© Kenneth Drake 1966
Reprinted 1967, 1970, 1972, 1973
Published in Great Britain by Studio Vista
35, Red Lion Square, London WCIR 4SG
and in America by Watson-Guptill Publications
1, Astor Plaza, New York, NY 10036
Library of Congress Catalog Card Number 66-13003
Set in Folio Grotesque 8 and 9 pt.
Printed in the Netherlands
by Grafische Industrie Haarlem B.V.
ISBN 0 289 36981 9

Contents

The author wishes to thank all
those numerous students, child
and adult, around whose
experience this book is written.

Pinched pot shapes

Foreword

The art of the potter has long been associated with the use of the potter's wheel for the making of thrown ware, and it continues to fascinate all who work with clay.

However, it is only a part of the story - a small part of the range of work open to the would-be potter. A little book cannot hope to do more than indicate some of the possibilities and show how the beginner can explore clay and develop fine satisfying work without the need for a potter's wheel.

There is little need for elaborate apparatus, and most of what you do need is easily improvised from quite normal household utensils.

The relationship between potter and clay is a very personal and intimate one. The deep pleasures and satisfactions which arise from a true understanding of the nature of the material are intangible but very real. Words cannot replace experience and understanding, and there is no substitute for handling clay. Clay is a unique material whose qualities are subtle and deserve understanding. This is fundamental if your relationship with clay is to be fruitful.

Since the handling of clay is so personal a matter, it would be inappropriate to provide a set of rules for making a variety of objects. Imitation may well be a sincere form of flattery, but in this context it is to be discouraged. You must work out your own solutions within your own limitations and your understanding of the behaviour of the clay.

This book does not set out to tell you what to make, but it suggests ways and means of arriving at a successful relationship with this most accommodating and fascinating material.

1 About clay

What it is

Clay is a special kind of earth which is made by the decomposition of rocks through the action of weathering agents. It has usually been carried from its point of origin by water, and deposited in beds where the water has run slackly. In the course of its travels the clay material has become much modified by many impurities, and the end product is very varied indeed. It is to be found almost everywhere and, though often very impure, may frequently be found in a sufficiently good state to prepare and use. Its preparation, though time consuming, is not difficult, and it is rewarding to have prepared and used your local clay.

Where to get it

You may, therefore, prepare your own clay from local resources, or purchase it from a potter's merchant or pottery supply house specialising in prepared clays. Local brickworks will often supply it cheaply, though probably some extra preparation may be needed before it is usable. It is worthwhile to keep an eye on building excavations, for they frequently expose excellent (and free) material. Not all clays are really suitable. Simple tests will help you to decide whether a particular one is worth using.

Take a lump the size of a fist from two or three feet down. (The top layers will probably be far too contaminated with rubble and top soil.) Allow it to dry thoroughly. Break it into small pieces in a basin and sprinkle it with water several times at intervals, so that it soaks up enough to soften it. Dry clay absorbs water much more easily than part dry clay. Take a little and knead it between your fingers until you have a ball of smooth clay. Take a small piece, round it into a ball, and observe whether it cracks easily at the edges. Roll a little sausage and coil it up. It should not break easily. Make a block about five inches long, an inch wide and half an inch thick. Mark five inches exactly and allow it to dry thoroughly. If it shows no sign of cracking or crumbling, has retained its shape and feels solid, it will probably do. Examine the five inch marks. If they now measure less than four and a half inches, the shrinkage is rather high and may lead to cracking and distortion in your work. The addition of a coarse material (sand, flint, or grog) may cure this and make it a good, workable material.

Clay direct from the supplier normally comes wrapped in plastic sheeting or plastic bags, and should be in good, usable condition. It should require no preparation at this stage, and may be left untouched for many months so long as it is properly covered and stored in a cool, frostproof place. The plastic sheeting or bag is invaluable for keeping work moist and should be carefully preserved. The clay may be supplied 'as dug', in which case you will have to prepare it as though you had dug it yourself. Clay is usually supplied in 1cwt lots in Great Britain and by the ton in the United States, but can, more expensively, be bought in smaller quantities.

All natural clays are improved by a long period of exposure to the weather, so that the variations of hot and cold, wet and dry can break down the lumps and render them easy to handle. There is also an improvement in the plasticity of the clay. However, this is by no means essential, and very satisfactory clay can be prepared in a few days in usable quantities.

You will, of course, choose clay as free from earth and stones as you can, and from as deep down as possible. It must be allowed to dry completely. This will take longer than you expect. Take it, a lump at a time, and crush it with a mallet, removing any stones and obvious impurities that emerge. This is best done in a shallow box to avoid scattering and wasting clay.

Remember - part dry clay is not only difficult to break up, but is reluctant to absorb water.

Have ready a tub with about an inch of water. When you have crushed each lump, sprinkle it into the tub until the water is all absorbed. Add another inch or so and continue until the tub is full. Leave it to soak for at least 48 hours. Longer is better.

You now have very soft, wet 'slurry' which must be dried sufficiently for subsequent preparation. This is best achieved by placing handfuls on to an absorbent surface - plaster slabs, clean bricks, concrete paving slabs. Do not be impatient. As it dries, it will free itself from the surface and may be lifted away, still very soft but ready to handle.

Now make a series of piles so that it can continue drying, but beware lest small pieces become hard. Control the drying with plastic sheeting or plastic bags.

a

b

c

d

Making ready for use

You need: solid work surface, clean and absorbent; cutting wire; scraper; moist cloth. Proceed as follows.

Rough mixing Take soft and harder clay alternately and slap down on to the bench firmly, one on the other, until you have a sandwich pile - say ten inches high (Fig. a). Use the cutting wire to slice down across the pile to make a new pile. Do this several times. It will mix and equalise the clay. Use the scraper to keep the bench clean. Little dry bits will destroy your hard work. Wipe drying clay from your hands.

Handwedging (Use this for small quantities.) Slice off (by hand or wire) a lump the size of two fists. Slap it into a round ball. Using a twisting, slicing movement, with the thumbs in opposite directions, halve the lump (Fig. b). Slap halves firmly together, changing direction of thumbs as you do so. Avoid sticking fingers into the clay, as this makes air pockets. Rotate clay so as to allow it to be sliced across the join. Repeat this slicing and smacking action a number of times, so as to make smooth and evenly mixed clay (Fig. c). A little practice will reveal the rhythm and produce results. This is best done with rather soft and plastic clay. The clay may now be used, or put into a larger pile to be bench wedged (Fig. d).

Bench wedging (For larger quantities.) After rough mixing or handwedging, make a pile about 12″ x 10″ x 4″. It will naturally stick to the bench, so coax it free and shape it somewhat by slapping and bumping on the bench. Finally, bump it firmly on the bench, leaving one end raised and near the edge of the bench. Use a cutting wire to slice upwards from the bench (Figs. a and b).

a

Place A on B and cut surfaces in line (Fig. c). Lift A high with both hands and smack it down firmly on to B, so as to explode air bubbles and make the clay adhere to itself. Use a firm rocking movement to coax the clay off the surface, taking care to avoid finger-marks and consequent air pockets. Slap it all round, and bump it a number of times to flatten it again. Turn it round and again place it firmly near the edge, with one end raised, so that it may again be cut up from underneath across the join. Repeat this cycle some ten or twelve times. This requires practice, but is necessary if your clay is to be in the best condition. During this time you will be able to find any stones or impurities.

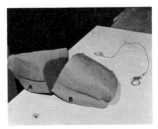

b

c

Points to watch

Keep the bench clear of clay bits. Use a scraper. Keep the clay surface smooth by slapping. Avoid all possibility of making air pockets.

Your aim To produce clay free from air pockets, having no stones or extraneous matter and evenly mixed.

d

Clay direct from the manufacturer, or prepared by yourself, will last indefinitely if it is closely wrapped in plastic sheeting or plastic bags. It is best stored in a cool place away from frost.

Prepared clay actually in use presents no problem if reasonable precautions are taken. Excellent rubbish bins (garbage cans) made of plastic, with close fitting lids, are now obtainable in a variety of colours and sizes. Prepared clay should be made into convenient balls and the bin kept full. Clay in bulk dries much more slowly. Cover it with plastic sheeting or plastic bags and keep the lid on.

The changing nature of clay

Clay rarely remains in a static condition. Its nature changes with its moisture content. Its physical properties and possibilities change progressively as it dries. It is named according to its changing state, and the names indicate definite stages, each with specific characteristics and possibilities.

Raw clay	Unprepared clay, generally in its natural state. Rarely capable of being used without further preparation. May be wet or dry, clean or dirty.
Slip or engobe	Clay and water mixed to produce a liquid which may be thick or thin. It is used decoratively as well as to assist in sticking clay together.
Slurry	Very thick slip verging on the plastic state. Used for sticking clay.
Plastic	Sufficiently hard and dry to allow modelling and manipulation generally. The starting point for most work with clay. Should not be sticky.
Leather hard	Partly dry, plastic clay. May be handled without fear of damage to the work. Will bend, but not easily break. Feels solid yet may still be cut, stamped, carved and stuck together with slip or slurry. Generally decorated with slip (engobe) or oxides at this stage.
Green or green ware	Generally refers to dry or unfired clay. Colour has changed, there is loss of weight.

It is very brittle, will not bend, and has shrunk in drying. It cannot be decorated or joined with slip. The chief decorative techniques involve oxides, wax, scraping and carving. It will break up in water and return to a slurry state. When thoroughly dried it may be fired.

Biscuit or bisque   This is the product of the first firing (from around 600° C upwards). Complete change of nature. Colour changes. Retains shape in water and is usually porous. May be decorated with combinations of oxide and glaze, using wax, sgraffito and painting techniques. Slip (engobe) cannot be used with it.

Glost   The final product. Biscuit, decorated and glazed, fired to the maximum temperature needed to melt the glaze.

Cycle of clay use

A natural cycle of clay preparation, use, and reconstitution follows if one understands the changing nature of the material.

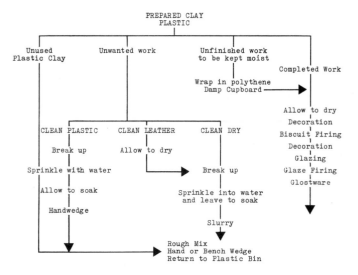

Although the catalogues will show a wide range of clays, your needs are simple. Most clays will fire to either a flower pot red or a buff colour, but they start life as a brown or grey colour. They are usually described as earthenware or stoneware clay, according to the normal maximum temperature to which they can be fired. They are usually supplied in a rather smooth, plastic condition which is more suitable for use on a potter's wheel. For many purposes this is quite suitable, though for handbuilt pottery coarser clay is not only more satisfactory to handle, but looks better. Coarser clays can be easily produced in the preparation stage by adding either:

> fireclay (a refractory clay)
> sand   (washed and clean)
> grog   (ground up biscuit).

Just mix handfuls into very wet clay at the 'rough mixing' stage and proceed to hand or bench wedge. The amount to add is best found by experiment. The resulting clay should still be plastic and pleasant to handle.

The addition of these materials not only makes a more satisfactory clay to handle, but reduces the amount of shrinkage in drying and so any tendency to warp and split.

Slip: how to prepare it, colour it and use it

To make slip (engobe) you sprinkle powdered clay into water until it will absorb no more. Leave it to soak a couple of days, then pass it through a 60 mesh sieve several times, using lots of water assisted by a brush. When it has settled, you can control the thickness by pouring off the excess water. In use you should keep it covered to prevent drying, and occasionally it should be resieved.

Since slip and clay must shrink the same amount, it is convenient to use powdered clay of the kind you work with. Most coloured slips (except black slip) are prepared from a light burning clay (usually ball clay), to which some body clay is added to help adjust its shrinkage rate to that of the clay in use. Colour is achieved by the use of natural clays which may be combined, or by the addition of metallic oxides in varying proportions. These are weighed and mixed dry with the powdered clay, and then sprinkled into water as for normal slip. A more complete mixture is made by separately grinding the oxide and then adding it to the slip.

Since slip is clay, and must therefore shrink as it dries, its uses are controlled by this shrinkage. It is *always* used in conjunction with *moist* (plastic or leather hard) clay, *never* on dry clay (dry clay plus wet slip = rapidly expanding clay = split pot) and *never* on fired (biscuit) pottery. (Fired clay which has ceased to shrink plus wet slip which must shrink = dry slip peeling off.) Even with moist clay, the slip decoration will occasionally peel off if the shrinkage rates of pot and slip are too different. This can usually be overcome by adding some of the body clay to the slip. To this end, make your basic slips of the same clay as the pot.

Slip may be applied decoratively in almost any manner you wish, and a good deal of experimentation is desirable. Every varying technique will produce its characteristic result whose qualities are worth investigation and decorative use. It may be brushed, poured, trailed, dipped into. Different colours may be applied at the wet stage, or later when it is dryer. It may be scraped off or resisted with wax or with paper (see p. 77). In fact, subject to the conditions already noted, it is a very versatile medium (see pp. 72-75).

Other uses

Slip is widely employed industrially in conjunction with plaster moulds for casting purposes. It is also used as an adhesive for clay.

Colour in slip (engobe)

Here are some starting points. The actual colours are greatly influenced by the kind of base clay used and the kind of glaze employed. Generally a transparent glaze is used, but others should be experimented with.

White natural ball clay
Cream 7/10 parts ball clay: 1 part red clay
Buff natural grey clay
Brown natural red/brown clay
Black red/brown clay 84% : manganese 6% : iron 10%
Green ball clay 98½% : copper oxide ½% : manganese oxide 1%
Blue ball clay 99% : cobalt oxide 1%

Once these have been made up, it is a good idea to mix them in specific proportions (spoonfuls, cupfuls etc.) to vary the range. Manufacturers also supply 'slip stains', but these should be used with great discretion as the colours may be far from pleasant.

2 Tools and equipment

With certain exceptions, these are very simple and can usually be contrived from normal household items. They fall into three general categories.

1 Large equipment

Kiln See p. 85.

Work bench This may be any solid table surface, preferably with a plain wooden top. Plastic surfaces are excellent for general use, but clay is inclined to stick during the wedging stage. A slightly absorbent surface is best. The heavier the table, the better.

Damp storage This is essential for work in progress and may be contrived in many ways. It is important to provide a damp atmosphere so as to retard the drying of the clay. Wooden cupboards can be rendered more efficient if the insides are lined with plastic sheeting, and better still if slabs of plaster (see pp. 48-9) are placed on the shelves and periodically soaked in water.

A good damp box may be contrived from an old water tank placed on its side, with shelves supported by bricks and again with plaster slabs to keep the atmosphere moist. The opening should be closely covered with plastic sheeting.

An excellent, small scale, damp cupboard can be made from a biscuit tin or bread box used upside down - especially if the lid is filled with plaster.

Plastic sheeting should, whenever possible, be wrapped around stored work to reduce the amount of dry air surrounding the clay. In emergency, or when work is too big for storage in the damp box, properly wrapped work can be retained for long periods quite safely. The work must, of course, be sufficiently hard to permit such wrapping.

Clay store By far the simplest way is to use plastic refuse bins (garbage cans), but any waterproof container, such as an old water tank, is excellent so long as it is kept well covered with plastic sheeting and is in a cool place. Keep the clay itself separately covered, to exclude as much air as possible.

2 General apparatus

Any number of bowls, basins, buckets, cannisters, jugs and funnels are wanted - preferably in good quality plastic, and with lids on where possible. Jars with screw-top lids are useful. Heavy duty floor cloths or rags are essential, and a large household cleaning sponge would be very valuable.

A wooden rolling pin with plain ends, some strips of wood ranging in thickness from $\frac{3}{8}''$ to $\frac{3}{4}''$ and 24" long (in pairs), and a piece of canvas or closely woven sacking (burlap) are needed for all the jobs requiring flat clay slabs.

Sieves are an essential item in the preparation of glazes and slips. They are described by diameter and by the number of holes per linear inch. Thus you will need two, 8" wide and of 60 and 120 mesh. These are made of phosphor bronze wire, finely woven, and are normally supplied ready fixed in round wooden frames. It is cheaper to buy the screen separately and make a square wooden frame yourself. A turntable is very valuable, but you can get along without it. A wire cake cooling tray is very useful for glazing. Get the strongest possible, big enough to fit across your largest basin. Some kind of water-jacket saucepan is needed to heat wax. A small glue pot, as used in woodwork and bookbinding, is excellent.

These are the bits and pieces that the potter finds useful and often makes for himself. Here are some examples whose uses will suggest themselves.

Cutting wire Traditionally, twisted string or wire is used for slicing clay. Thick nylon fishing line is a good substitute. Use brass curtain rings, toggle buttons, or large buttons for handles. Secure the loose ends with a flame.

Pricker (Pin) A common hat pin, stuck through a cork, is excellent.

Knife A pocket knife with the blade ground thin and pointed, or any thin bladed knife 4″-6″ long.

Scrapers These take many forms. Each is very useful for particular purposes.

a. Flexible metal scraper with rounded edges. For smoothing, scraping and controlling built shapes.

b. Kidney presser. Similar in shape to a. but made of firm rubber with tapered edges. Used on soft clay.

c. House-painter's scraper. Excellent for cleaning up the bench.

d. e. Tooth-edged scrapers. Made from broken hack-saw blade and metal adhesive spreader. Used to smooth rough surfaces and to create texture.

f. A piece of rasp plane blade.

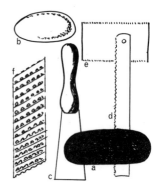

Bats Any surface used to carry pottery around is a 'bat'. Squares which are cut from hardboard or asbestos-cement sheeting are ideal. Have plenty of them, ranging in size from 6″ to at least 24″ across.

Sponges Small, natural, close-textured sponges are very useful for cleaning and damping work in progress, and for general wiping in all cases requiring particular delicacy. Synthetic sponges in a variety of shapes are also available and generally used.

Brushes Almost any brush has its use in pottery, and many special types have been evolved. However, for brushing glaze or slip through a sieve, use a domestic nylon pot scourer. Also illustrated are a 'mop' and a 'pencil'. You need a variety of kinds and shapes, and you can manage quite well using normal household painting brushes, watercolour (sable or camel) brushes, and one or two hoghair (bristle) brushes.

Slip trailers Many versions of the slip trailer exist. Two types are normally in use, both specially made for the purpose: (a) a soft, flat, rubber bag which is filled by means of a funnel and (b) a bulb-shaped trailer which is filled by first squeezing all the air out and then allowing the slip to be sucked in. Nozzles of both glass and plastic are available.

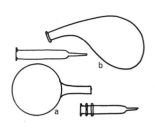

Modelling tools All kinds are very useful, but particularly those with wire loops of varying shapes. Generally these are supplied with smooth wires. It is a good plan to use the edge of a file to make a series of teeth, so that they scrape and cut more efficiently and leave a pleasant texture on the surface of the clay.

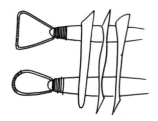

3 Beginning with clay (1)

Right handling and understanding of the material

Your aim is to submit the clay to trial by fire. Give it the best chance of survival by right handling, by understanding how it behaves and by responding to its varying moods and possibilities. Do not try to impose your will on it, but rather submit to its disciplines. Discover its strengths and weaknesses. Try not to bring preconceived notions of how it ought to behave, but rather bring a receptive, questing mind to the business of exploring these disciplines and so establish a personal relationship with clay. Right handling plus understanding gives the right result.

You have spent a good deal of time and energy in preparing your clay, making it free from pockets of air, from unequal lumps, and getting it to the right degree of plasticity. Be fully aware of this from now on. No unnecessary finger-marks which can cause air pockets. No bits of clay left around to dry hard and get mixed with your moist clay. No moist clay pointlessly drying and spoiling (always cover it up with a moist cloth) and, above all, remember the 'clayness' of clay.

Exploration and techniques

You can pass this by if you are impatient, but it's worthwhile exploring thoughtfully like this.

Slapping and shaping Take a fist-sized lump of clay. Slap it between the hands. Round it up. Continue to slap, changing the form of the clay as you do so. Change the nature of your slapping. Use, perhaps, the side of your hand. Build up a collection of slapped shapes. Do they reflect the way of making as well as the shape of the hand? Could they have been made in some other way? Are they satisfying shapes? Do they exist as shapes in their own right, or do they reflect other ideas?

Rotation Take some smaller bits of clay and begin to explore ways of rolling them between the palms of the hands. The shapes made will reflect the varying kinds of pressures and rotations you make (Fig. a). Build up a collection of shapes which express the different qualities of rotation. Do the same thing once more, this time using the fingertips only. See how the techniques change. Examine them as shapes. Do they have a right or less right point of view? Considerations of design are always implicit in all you do.

a

Beating or paddling Try another ball. This time find out ways of modifying its shape by gentle bumping or tapping on the bench. Once more make a collection of flattened shapes, some having very few surfaces, others as complicated as you can (Fig. c). Find out what behaves best - rather moist clay or clay that has dried somewhat. Find the limitations and scope of this.

b

Find a bit of wood and use it to beat or paddle your clay (Fig. d). This is quite a different matter and needs different consideration. Not only will you be making flattened surfaces (which may give way to rounded forms), but you will leave the marks of beating or paddling behind. Look at these. They may be haphazard, but can be controlled too. Look at them in relation to the shape being made. Use them consciously.

c

d

Squeezing and pinching Take some more clay. Slap or bump it into a satisfying shape. Now begin to modify its surface by carefully pinching up the clay so as to use the existing shape and so as to change its nature. There are lots of ways of pinching and squeezing. Try this: take a ball in one hand and grip it tightly so that your fingers dig into it. You have made a special shape characteristic of your hand. Release your fingers carefully and consider the form you have made; now gently begin to modify the shape by pinching or nipping. Here is a very different kind of form using the *inside* of your ball of clay. Explore this notion to find out how far you can control the shapes you make. How much will the clay stand? Was the clay too soft? Ought you to have allowed it to dry a little before going on? Continue to work with other clay to make shapes *from the inside*. These shapes will naturally be of a particular kind, as the result of a particular activity. The means of working the clay dictates the end product.

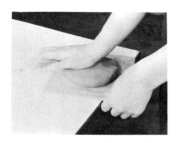

Flat clay You must explore some of the possibilities of making flat clay in your hands. Extend the range of your experience by working the clay to its limits. Find out how far you really can go.

Using your finger-tips only, take a piece of clay and manipulate it until you have a good ball. Then, rotating and squeezing, make it into as flat and thin a disc as you can. Don't forget to keep your fingers clean and moist. Dry hands produce dry, cracked clay. You ought to achieve wafer thinness before it breaks.

Try a slightly larger (orange size) piece. Begin to pat and rotate it between the palms, keeping it vertical. Make it as flat and large as possible.

Again, take an average sized ball. Slap it into a good, round shape. Place it on a small (6" x 6") bat near the edge of the bench so that you can turn the bat round easily.

Use the heel of the hand to press it repeatedly while turning the bat round. The aim is to keep it as flat as possible - edges and middle alike. It may stick to the bat. Every now and then gently release it and carry on.

As you explore both clay and techniques, be concerned about the forms you are creating. Let them express the qualities of the techniques you have been exploring, always with regard to what happens to the clay. Is it too wet? Is it too dry? Are your hands moist and clean? Have you got bits of dry clay lying around? Is your unused clay spoiling? Have you kept it properly covered?

Make a series of flat slabs and consider the possibilities of enlivening the surface. The mere act of making the slabs has already made some surface pattern and texture. Develop this idea by deliberately making marks, random or organised. Find out how many ways you can create interesting texture by using your hands only, your fingers, your knuckles, your nails. Pinch or press the clay freely, in organised lines, circles, spirals. Drag your fingers. Raise the surface up or lower it. Make a series of separate or related tiles. Develop this idea by making a panel (see pp. 49-50).

Look around for other ways to make pattern and texture by stamping. Search out any object that will make a mark - a piece of wood, a cotton reel (spool), a key and so on. Find out how many different ways these will make marks. Use them to make formal patterns as well as free textures. Almost anything will do, and will have as personal a mark as a fingerprint.

Next, make your own stamps from clay and explore them. They are easily made from a roll of clay (finger thick), cut into suitable lengths and given various forms by rolling or beating so as to make round, oval, square or triangular sections.

Marks may be pressed into the ends or along the sides with any interesting tool, and when they have hardened, they can be rolled and pressed in many ways. A stick of chalk may also be used in the same way.

Clay applied to the surface provides a wide range of possibility. The surface must be fairly moist. Try applying little pellets of clay, or little coils of clay. Use them separately or in combination. Use varying sizes in combination, thick rolls alongside thin ones, large pellets against small ones and so on. Apply the clay so as to retain the pellet or roll-like character (gentle flat pressure), or deliberately smear the edges downwards so as to lose the original form. Try applying a different colour.

When the clay is harder, try making carved marks too, and when it is really dry inscribe textures by scratching.

These and many other ideas that you will develop for yourself are not only interesting exercises, but are intimately concerned in all surface decoration over the whole ceramic range. These may be accepted as individual pieces of work, or collectively may be made into panels. They may be completed by being fired and then mounted, or they may be cast in plaster or used with the sand-casting process.

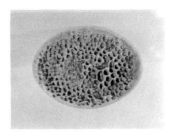

Finger texture

Found' stamps

Stamps and roulettes

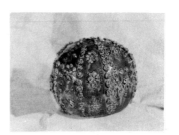

Applied clay

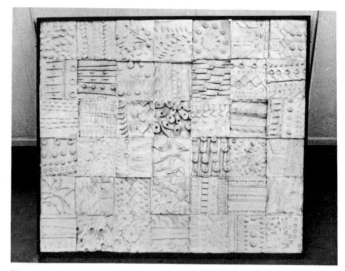

Plaster panel: 'found' textures. Made by adult.

Joining clay

You will avoid much disappointment if you consider care-fully the joining processes.

Soft plastic clay of course sticks readily to itself and, so long as you avoid trapping air in the joins, will give little trouble. Beware, however, of merely touching the pieces together. They may seem to stick, but on drying will shrink away from each other. It is always wise to smear the actual join over. Avoid much pressing as this will tend to spoil the shape of your work.

Slightly harder clay is best joined by moistening the sur-faces with slip. Wipe it off and then press firmly together. The edges are then smeared over.

Soft leather clay joins well if a little thick slip is used as glue. The joins must be smeared over.

Hard leather clay will require the surfaces scratched or scored thoroughly, and then thick slip rubbed in and wiped away to leave a sticky surface before the clay is pressed together and the edges sealed off.

It is not worthwhile to try to stick dry clay, because the shrinkage rates are such that the joins must inevitably come apart.

4 Beginning with clay (2)

Here are some techniques which you will need all the time.

1 Rolled flat clay

You need: rolling pin (without handles if possible), canvas cloth or burlap, strips of wood of various thicknesses, pricker pin and clay. You will save much time and frustration if you forget pastry rolling techniques at the outset. Use well prepared clay which has been given a somewhat flattened shape.

Fig. a The sticks are only necessary if you must have a slab of a definite, even thickness. They are very useful while you gain confidence. First of all flatten the lump somewhat by slapping it, but remember that it will quickly stick to the canvas or burlap, and cannot therefore move across its surface.

a

Fig. b By placing one hand on the clay while lifting the canvas with the other, the clay and canvas can be separated. This must be done frequently as the rolling progresses. Never try to lift the clay by its edge.

b

Fig. c Place sticks in position and start rolling *from the middle, once in each direction.* More than this is a waste of time, as the clay sticks to the canvas or burlap. Release the clay every time you roll. Change the direction of rolling every time if you want a round shape, and start with a long shape rolled in one direction only if you want a long narrow shape. Roll up to the edges only.

c

Strength through structure

Soft clay at this stage has little strength and is unable to support its own weight. It can, however, be endowed with remarkable structural strength if properly handled. You should now explore ways of exploiting this.

If you cut some simple rectangular strips and attempt to stand them on end, they will collapse. On their sides they will possibly survive. In this sideways position join a couple along their length and try again. Create a variety of girder-like forms using strips joined at right angles, and assemble them to make complex structures. Add horizontals as well as verticals and concentrate on making structures to express this flat angularity. Try to construct tall shapes, which must be structurally sound to survive.

Take a sheet of clay with one straight side and try to stand it up. It will collapse, but as soon as you fold it in gentle curves it will survive. Explore the limits of this. How thin can you go and still make it stand securely? Roll a cylinder round the rolling pin and it will stand. Slice it in half and it still has strength. Even in quarters it will have strength. Begin to assemble these part cylinders into structures designed to give support to each other. Try making cone shapes as well.

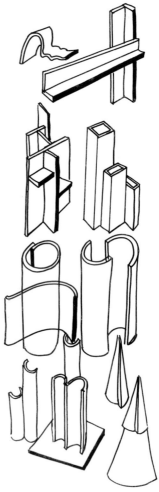

You will find limitations in yourself as well as in the clay. Give yourself a real chance. Make good joins and always work on a bat so that you can carry it around.

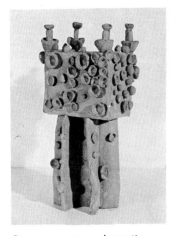

Strong structure: decorative
use of applied clay.
Made by child.

Tall structure from curved clay.
Made by adult.

Other developments from flat clay

Tiles: wide variety possible, including modelling in high
relief and the addition of cut flat clay forms, panels
and mosaics (pp. 60-2).

Dishes: moulded (hump or hollow) (pp. 39, 40, 42, 44).

Slab pottery: boxes, bottles, tray shapes (pp. 64-5).

Sculptural forms.

Simple modelling using folded forms (p. 69).

A special point about tile making For most slab work it is
not very necessary for the clay to dry absolutely flat, but
for tiles it is. It is necessary therefore to get the clay to dry
equally from both sides, so that shrinkage will produce
equal stresses on both sides. One very good system is to
make a series of flat plaster slabs and to stack tiles and
plaster sandwich fashion so that the water dries out evenly.
This needs to be done very slowly (p. 48).

There are two ways of making clay ropes, coils or rolls, both of which call for a good deal of practice. It is desirable to be able to make them quickly and in quantity. If you are slow, the clay will dry and crack and be generally difficult to handle. Hands should be kept moist and clean, and for bench rolling the bench must be kept moist too. Use good, well prepared clay.

Hand coiling Once you have gained control of this method, you will find that this is a quick and easy way of making ropes, but it is possibly the more difficult of the two. Take a fist-sized ball of clay - slap it into a round and then a pear shape. Then, with the whole hand, begin to squeeze it, turning it as you do so. It is important to keep the fingers close together so as to avoid uneven pressures and the resulting string of sausages. Use both hands, turning and squeezing, so that the clay extrudes from below the hands in an even rope. From time to time, reverse the clay and never allow it to dangle over the top of the hand. If your result is a little unequal, you can of course roll it on the bench, but this is not really desirable.

Bench rolling Begin with well prepared clay and slap and squeeze it into a fairly even thick rope, making it as round as you conveniently can. Avoid bumping it on the bench, as this will make a flat side which will be difficult to get rid of. See that the bench has no bits of drying clay and that it is moist. Rolling takes a lot of water out of the clay, causing it to crack. With both hands, fingers outspread, begin to roll the clay to and fro, using as much bench as possible. As the clay becomes round, increase pressures and move outwards from the middle. The fingers never remain in the same spot for more than a moment or two, and constantly work from the middle outwards. Watch the ends and keep them the same thickness as the middle. If a flat side develops, pick the rope up and carefully hand coil until it is round again.

Development Clay ropes are used particularly for making coiled pots. They are more suitable for fairly large pots, and some forms of modelling make use of them. Occasionally handles are made from coils.

Hand coiling

Bench rolling

3 Pulled clay

This technique is the one normally used for making the handles on wheel-made pots, but it can be applied to handbuilt pottery too in a number of ways. It involves coaxing the clay out from the main lump by a stroking, pulling movement.

a

Fig. a Take a fist-sized lump of well prepared clay and slap it from a round into a pear shape, accentuating the small end into an elongated tail.

Have a basin of water handy. Wet the clay and your hand and, using a pulling, coaxing movement, extend the tail gradually. Keep the lump turning as you pull and take care to taper the shape gently.

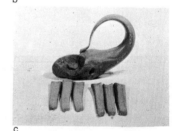
b

Fig. b At this stage it may be flattened by working on alternate sides. Interesting ridges and depressions can be made by using the thumb to groove as the pulling continues.

Fig. c When a satisfactory length and shape has been made, it may be curved back on to its lump to harden off for subsequent use, or it may be pinched off and placed flat on a bat until it is harder.

c

Fig. d Feet are often added using this simple technique. Four equal balls of clay are prepared and made into a little cone shape in the fingers. Then, with a little slip and a thumb, they are gently pressed home and the join smeared over. Now, using the pulling technique, they are gently coaxed into a taller cone shape

d

of the required length. The shape should taper to its point and join the pot with a smoothly rounded curve.

Coiled pot: beaten and stamped. Fired, glazed and scraped, fired. Made by adult.

Coiled pot: beaten and textured. Fired, glazed and refired. Made by adult.

Coiled pot: surface scraped smooth, incised, oxided and re-scraped. Made by adult.

Coiled pot: applied clay to emphasise light and shade. Surface texture direct from the hand. Made by adult.

Coiled pot: unfired pot waxed and oxided. Fired pot waxed, glazed and waxed again under second glaze.

Coil pot: two joined 'upside down' coil pots. Surface roughened with sand and slip. Oxide rubbed onto dry pot. Thinly glazed with matt transparent glaze. Made by adult.

5 Plaster and mouldmaking

Plaster slabs and various kinds of plaster mould are easy to make and invaluable. Plaster, however, needs handling with care. You can get different grades of plaster which set at varying speeds. The potter's merchant or pottery supply house usually specifies 'potter's plaster'. This sets fairly slowly and allows you time to work in an unhurried way. It is cheaper bought by the hundredweight or 100 lb bag, and should preferably be stored in a waterproof container in a dry place. Like this it will remain in good condition for long periods.

Special points

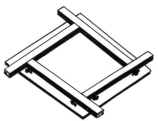

1 On no account pour any plaster, plaster water or waste into the sink. It will set and block the drains.
2 Do not allow plaster and clay to get mixed if you intend to use the clay for pot making. Keep separate clay for all plaster work.
3 Make all your preparations before you begin to mix the plaster.
4 Use *dry* hands in the plaster powder.
5 If your hands are sensitive, use a barrier cream or, just as effectively, rub them with ordinary, thin machine oil.
6 For unmessy results be organised and unhurried.
7 Prepare to deal with unwanted plaster. To begin with you must estimate the amount needed. You will probably make too much. This can be useful. Use a smooth flat surface (a sheet of glass is excellent), and arrange four strips of wood in the way shown. Fix them with some clay and use this mould for your excess plaster. It makes very good plaster bats, having a glazed surface. Alternatively, keep a supply of plastic bags handy. Pour the excess plaster in and hang them up to set. The resulting shapes are very interesting as starting points for carving.

If you didn't make enough plaster the first time, wash the basin thoroughly and start again. If possible, 'rough up' the surface of the first plaster before adding more.

Mixing plaster
Arrange your work in sequence.

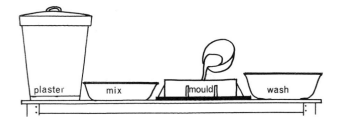

1 Choose an unchipped enamel bowl or one of plastic, with a fairly flat base. Put some water in (say half full). Always allow space for the plaster to be added.

2 With *dry hands* scoop up the plaster powder and sprinkle it into the water. Sift it through the fingers freely and rapidly, but *do not dump it* into the water ... this makes lumpy plaster. Continue like this until an island of dry plaster appears on the surface and is not readily absorbed (Fig. a).

3 At this point, slide your hand down the side of the basin so that it rests *flat* on the bottom. Wriggle your hand vigorously to mix the plaster. Properly done, this will produce a definite circulatory movement which will not only avoid air bubbles but make an even mix without splashing. Once a creamy mix is evident, use it without delay. Your plaster is already beginning to set (Fig. b).

4 An old 4″ or 6″ rubber ball cut in half makes an excellent flexible scoop which allows plaster to be poured with precision. Together with a rubber kidney presser it is also an excellent tool for cleaning out the basin afterwards.

5 Immediately you have poured the plaster into the mould, transfer everything to the washing up basin (not the sink). This water must be allowed to stand a while to let the plaster settle to the bottom. Excess water can be gently poured off. The sludge is left to harden and dry, when it may be collected and thrown away.

Simple plaster dish moulds

Moulded dish shapes are the starting point for numerous pottery activities. There are two kinds of shapes with various names:

A. Press-in or hollow.
B. Flop-over, mushroom or hump.

Both have the same starting point: a solid clay master form.

First considerations In designing a mould you should remember that the dish is not an end in itself, but a starting point for further activity. It must therefore be conceived in simple terms, with a shape conditioned by the nature of the tools and by the way it is made. To try to make a complicated shape, with acute angles, absolute symmetry, or straight lines would not only be technically difficult, but would limit its further development.

Paper pattern Make a pattern with smoothly curved lines and no acute angles anywhere. These may be free forms, or a certain symmetry may be given by first folding the paper so as to achieve a balanced shape. Tough paper is best.

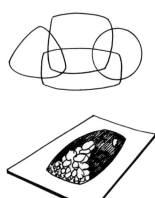

The master shape (press-in mould) Choose a flat, smooth surface (thick glass, plastic, sheet metal). Allow 3"-4" free space all round. Put the paper pattern down and hold it down with a few lumps of clay. Now build up a solid shape which is your dish shape upside down. Use large pieces of clay for the middle and grade them off for the edges. Air pockets are not important, but a good profile shape is. Keep a careful watch on both the plan and the profile shape. This need not be symmetrical, but should have a good line. As the shape you want emerges, use finer and finer pellets to fill in the hollows.

Once the shape is fairly sure, you can let it dry a little. Stiffer clay is easier to handle. However careful you have been, the surface will still need a good deal of working over (Fig. a). Using a toothed scraper, begin to scrape in constantly changing directions. In this way you will quickly remove the high spots and expose the hollows. Fill the hollows with more pellets of clay and continue alternately to scrape and fill. Once in a while use the flexible metal scraper to smooth the surface. See that you use the scraper on edge so as to really scrape. The painter's scraper may be effectively used round the edges both to define the outline and to establish the angle of it (Fig. b).

Watch the edges very carefully to ensure that there is no overhang which would prevent the mould and dish from separating easily (Fig. c).

As the clay dries, your work will become more precise. When you finally use a smooth scraper, the surface should be really free from bumps and have a clean outline. There is no need for the clay to dry entirely.

Next you must build a wall round the master form (Fig. d). This is conveniently done with clay, though substitutes such as a strip of linoleum or an old piece of machine belt can

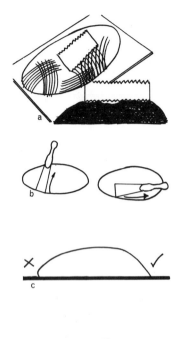

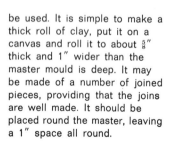

be used. It is simple to make a thick roll of clay, put it on a canvas and roll it to about $\frac{5}{8}''$ thick and 1" wider than the master mould is deep. It may be made of a number of joined pieces, providing that the joins are well made. It should be placed round the master, leaving a 1" space all round.

Make sure it sits firmly down on the base. Keep the edges as tidy as possible (no finger-marks etc.), and check the joins again. Use any spare clay to make buttresses on the outside (Fig. e). Nothing is worse than a flood of half set plaster.

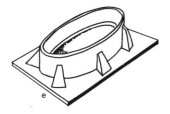

Mix the plaster and, using the half rubber ball scoop, begin gently to pour it over the master shape so as to cover it first. Then, keeping an eye on the speed of the setting plaster, more rapidly fill up the rest of the space. Do this cautiously, or the sudden influx of plaster may cause the walls to give way.

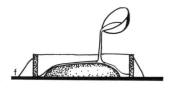

In about fifteen minutes the plaster will be well set (and will have developed quite a lot of heat). You should now remove the clay walls and wrap them in plastic sheeting for subsequent use. None of this should be mixed with normal clay again. Rough edges should be pared off (a rasp tooth plane is excellent). There may be a little difficulty in removing the whole mould from its base, but this can usually be overcome by turning it all upside down on to a couple of bricks, over a pad of cloth, and gently bumping the back. Don't be in a hurry. Carefully dig out the clay form (don't use metal tools which will damage the new plaster) and wrap it up with the walls. Wash in cold water.

You now have a press-in or hollow mould.

It is a good idea to plane off one edge to make a flat base for easy storage.

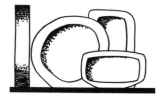

Master moulds:

the use of templates

Some alternative ideas for
master mould making are worth
noting. If you want a form
which has an exact profile
shape all round, it is useful to
make a template. Cardboard
will do, but it is worthwhile to
make a more permanent one in
aluminium or tin sheet, as they
can be used repeatedly. In the
case of the cardboard template,
its use would be restricted to
testing the profile shape, but a
metal template is used to
actually scrape away the clay.

This is much more controlled
if, instead of making a paper
pattern for the basic form, the
shape is cut from thin plywood
or hardboard. It is particularly
useful if the same basic shape
is to be made a number of
times. This hardboard pattern
becomes a template too, so that
the profile and base shapes
work together.

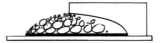

Clay is built up on the base
pattern as before, with the
frequent use of the template to
scrape away excess clay.
Hollows are filled with pellets
and so on until a smooth and
accurate surface is obtained.

Note: it is very necessary to
see that the edges of both the
metal template and the base
hardboard are accurate
and smooth.

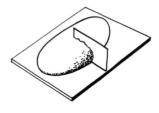

Using a 'press-in' mould

Roll out a slab of clay using a canvas cloth, rolling pin and guide sticks. The thickness required will vary with the size of the dish. It should also be remembered that the clay will shrink too. For a small (6") dish use $\frac{1}{4}$" sticks, and for a large one (18") $\frac{1}{2}$" guides.

Select and clean your mould with a moist sponge. Keep it dry if possible, and never scrape it in case you damage the plaster surface. Place the mould face down on to the clay, which must be trimmed so as to leave about $\frac{3}{4}$" spare all round. Remove the mould and release the clay from the canvas or burlap.

Line up mould and clay so that the mould can be lifted to the vertical position with the left hand. Raise the clay (on a cloth) on to the right hand. Peel off the cloth. Raise up the mould and clay together. Lower them down so the clay drops into the mould. For little dishes this procedure is not vital, but with large slabs it is very necessary.

By carefully lifting the edges, coax the clay down into the mould. Trim the clay a little so as to leave about 1" standing up all round. Do not let the clay flop down over the edges.

Now drip a little water into the mould and, using a clean, moist kidney presser, begin to coax the clay to fit the shape. *Always work from the middle outwards* and in all directions, so that you do not trap air between the clay and the mould (with consequent cracks at a later stage).

It will require some practice to be able to leave the surface free from marks, but as long as you keep the presser at a fairly oblique angle as it touches the clay, it should not be too difficult. It is all made easier by having it on a turnable. Try not to use a sponge. It leaves a rather unsatisfactory surface.

The waste clay at the edge can now be trimmed off with a needle, a cutting wire, or a 'frog', which is a wire stretched catapult fashion. The wire or needle must be kept flat on the edge of the plaster to ensure a good finish.

At this point the inside edge can be smoothed off with a clean, wet finger. The outer edge is left until the clay is removed from the mould at the leather hard stage. The clay can then be planed with a toothed rasp plane blade and sponged.

While the clay is still in the mould, it is ready for development and decoration.

Since the mould is providing support for the very soft, moist clay, wet techniques such as the use of slip, or the application of clay, are particularly suitable.

If the press-in is considered as a negative, then the mush-room is a positive taken from the negative (press-in) mould. The mould selected should be clean and free from bits of dry clay etc. It should be placed on its back as level as possible. If necessary, a spirit level can be used and little pellets of clay put under the mould to make it level and secure. The inside and the top edges must be covered with thin ball clay slip, which can be painted on with a soft-haired brush, or poured in, swirled round carefully and poured out in such a way as to cover the top edges at the same time. While this is setting somewhat, prepare a quant-ity of plaster.

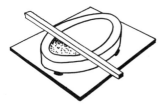

As the plaster begins to thicken, scoop some up with the half ball and pour gently. A strong stream may wash away the ball clay slip, so be careful. Fill the mould until it is slightly overflowing, and then level off the surface with a strip of wood.

When the plaster has hardened, scratch the middle area well so as to provide a key for subsequent plaster. Roll out some clay, and build a 3″ high wall round the scratches so as to leave about 1½″ clear round the outside of the wall. Fill with plaster and allow it to set. Remove the clay wall and tidy up the stalk thus formed.

When it has had time to set well (say 24 hours), the two parts must be separated. This is usually done by a prolonged soaking in water. It is assisted by placing the inverted mould on to blocks at its outside edges, with some cloths below to minimise the damage if the halves part suddenly. It is also possible to exert a strong downwards pull to aid the process. But be patient.

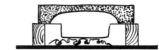

42 The final stage comes after the mould has been cleaned up. In order to strengthen the edge and to provide a cutting guide for trimming the clay later, it is usual carefully to bevel the edge to an angle of about 45°. This is best done with a rasp plane blade.

Using a mushroom mould

Clay must be rolled out as for the press-in mould, and left on its canvas cloth or burlap. A rough estimate of the area needed can be made by placing the mould (stalk side up) on to the slab, and gently lifting the canvas or burlap up, so that the clay presses slightly on the edge of the mould. This, repeated at intervals, will give a good idea of size. Trim to 1″ outside this line.

Drag the clay on its canvas or burlap on to a board and place the mould in position. With one hand supporting the mould, and one under the board, reverse the whole thing. Remove the board and peel off the canvas cloth to leave the clay draped over the mould. Lift the mould and clay on to a turntable, cover the clay with a moist cloth and gently begin to coax the clay down and round the mould, starting from the middle. A suitably chosen cloth will impress an attractive

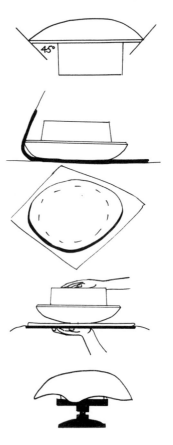

texture on to the back, or alternatively, a suitably used kidney presser, working from the middle out, will make. a very smooth surface.

Particular care needs to be taken to avoid finger-marks or nipping the clay off on the edge of the mould.

If you have checked to see
that the clay really fits the
mould, trim off the excess with
a needle. A knife is not very
satisfactory. It is best
accomplished in two stages.
First trim with the needle
level with the underside of
the mould, and then find the
angle of the bevelled edge
and trim at that angle.

The outside edge may now
be rounded with a moist finger
and sponged. The inner edge
is dealt with when the clay
has hardened to leather hard
and is removed from the mould.

Before the clay is left to
harden, it is essential to release
the edges from the mould so
that the clay can shrink without
danger of splitting itself.

While the clay is still on the
mould, it is often appropriate
to add feet by using the pulled
clay technique. Alternatively a
foot ring can be added by
making a rope of clay which is
joined to the dish by smearing.

With both the press-in and
the mushroom moulds, final
drying is best done with the
dish upside down on a flat
board, as this minimises
warping and splitting.

The mushroom mould lends
itself to a special form of
decoration in which the surface
of the plaster mould is carved,
so that when clay is pressed
over it, the hollow carving
results in a raised pattern on
the inside of the dish. The
plaster is easily carved with a
lino cutting tool.

Apart from their obvious uses as dishes, with or without feet and rings, these moulds can be used in a variety of ways. Here are some of the more direct developments:-

1 *Built up dishes* The clay slab, slightly more substantial than usual, is pressed into the mould and the edges are built up by the addition of ropes of clay as for a coiled pot, or flat slabs are prepared and set upright on the edges of the moulded dish. In both cases the joins must be very well done. When the clay is hard enough, remove it from the mould. Special attention must be given to ensuring that the outside joins are well sealed off.

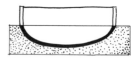

2 *Joined dishes* Interesting forms can be made by joining identical dishes face to face, and these shapes can be used for subsequent development.

A dish is pressed into a mould and the edges trimmed flat. A board is placed over the mould and the whole turned upside down. At the earliest moment, when the clay comes away from the mould, the mould can be reused, leaving an undamaged dish to harden upside down on the board.

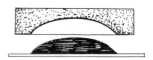

The second dish is pressed into the mould at once and left to harden somewhat. When both halves are hard enough to handle, a thin roll of very soft clay is placed on the edge of the dish in the mould, and the first half carefully placed and

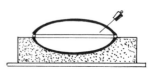

pressed down on top. They are now left to get harder.

There is now a large volume of air contained within, and it is necessary to make an air hole to equalize the air pressures.

Built up moulded dish: heavily grogged clay, oxided, inside scraped. Made by adult.

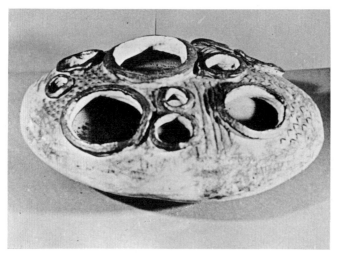

Double dish shape: holes cut and built up. Made by child.

Double dish bottle: top made from cut off base, oxided and scratched. Made by adult.

Double dish bottles: neck coiled. Made by adult.

Double dish form: pressed decoration, coiled foot. Made by adult.

According to the shapes involved, interesting developments can be made by cutting and re-assembling the pieces, or by building on to them. For example, bottle and similar forms might be made by cutting a slice from one end and replacing it on the other.

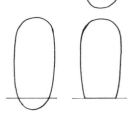

The neck, of course, would be built up as for a coiled pot (see p. 53), and a flat slab is needed for the base.

Other ideas to explore include such things as panels whose surface could employ cut sections from dish shapes (see p. 61), as well as modelling possibilities.

The full range of decorative possibility should be explored. The following notes will suggest some appropriate lines to follow for both press-in and mushroom moulds.

Soft plastic clay   fluid slip (dripped, splashed, poured, brushed, trailed, etc.).

Dryer, but still
  plastic clay   tissue paper resist with poured slip. Poured slip, allowed to harden and scraped. Applied clay (ridges and balls applied). Pressed decoration (fingers, found objects and specially made roulettes and stamps). Use of slips and oxides. Scrape off when dry.

Nearly dry/dry clay   lines incised with any sharp instrument (paint with oxide and scrape surface). Oxide whole areas and scrape design with a variety of different instruments. Use hot wax, oxide over, re-wax and oxide again. Use cold candle or wax crayon with oxide.

Some techniques are specially suitable for use with the mushroom mould. These must be done while the clay is still flat on the canvas or burlap, and subsequently placed on the mould when the decoration is sufficiently set. This applies particularly to slip trailing and decoration generally, and also to pressed and stamped decorations (see p. 74).

Flat plaster slabs

Really flat tiles are difficult to make unless they can be dried equally from both sides at the same time. The solution lies in very flat, smooth slabs of plaster. By arranging the clay sandwich fashion between dry plaster slabs, and allowing a slow drying period, this is not at all difficult. Clay with a high percentage of stiffening material (grog, sand, flint, or fireclay) is best.

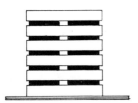

Materials Three pieces of moulding made as shown in the diagram.
One length of strong string.
Two pieces of heavy glass cut accurately to size - in this case 9″ x 8½″.

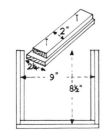

Assemble the glass and framing as shown, and bind them by wrapping the string round. The glass may be held tightly by wedging pieces of wood between the glass and the string.

Fill up with plaster and level off at the top as it begins to set.

Allow it time to set and then remove the glass. You will have glassy smooth plaster.

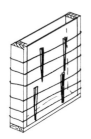

Rolled out tiles: dried between plaster. Manganese and iron oxide, scraped, transparent shining glaze. Made by children.

Heavily grogged clay, carved, oxided, fired, glazed and scraped, then refired with melted coloured glass. Made by adult.

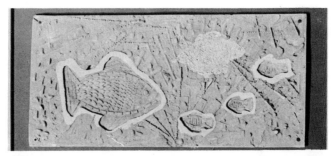

Sandcasting: thin stamped clay fish shapes, individually plaster cast, embedded in moist sand before casting. Group work by children.

Sandcasting: clay spirals fired. Used to stamp moist sand, then embedded before casting. Made by adult.

Sandcasting: 'found' shapes stamped into moist sand before casting. Made by adult.

Further plaster slabs

A useful piece of equipment,
very simply made, is an
adjustable frame made from
four pieces of wood and four
angle irons. The diagram shows
how to assemble it. The same
system is used for larger
frames for special purposes,
but without the angle irons.
It is quite satisfactory to use
clay to hold the wood in
position. The frame is very
useful for making panels
incorporating ceramic pieces
(tesserae), or any other items
such as pebbles, bits of mirror,
items of plastic, etc.

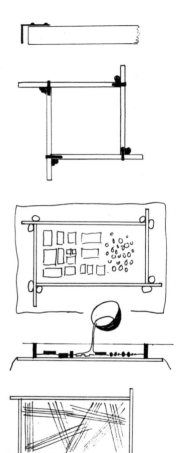

Spread a large plastic sheet
on the table. Next arrange the
frame with the correct internal
sizes, and fix from the outside
with wads of clay. Cover the
inside space with $\frac{1}{2}''$ of *moist*
clean sand. You can now make
your design by pressing into
the sand so as to leave marks
and textures (every grain of
sand will make its presence
felt). Or you can place ceramic
pieces, mosaic tesserae,
pebbles, bits of plaster, wood,
or glass face down on the
sand . . . or into the sand.
Varying depths are very
interesting.

Strips of plasterer's scrim
(2" wide x 12"-15"), or
loose weave burlap, are cut
as reinforcement.

The plaster is mixed and
poured very gently from the
half rubber ball, taking great
care not to disturb the sand.
As soon as the surface is
covered, dip the scrim or burlap

into the plaster and
spread it over, patting it
carefully. Overlap the scrim or
burlap in varying directions.
A little more plaster is then
floated over it all. There is no
need to make a thick layer, as
reinforced plaster is surprisingly
strong.

Glazed slabs and tesserae set with plaster. Made by child.

The plaster should be allowed to set very solidly before it is disturbed. When the surrounding wooden frame is removed, the plastic sheeting which keeps the bench clean can conveniently be used to lift the slab and so expose the sand, most of which can now be scraped off. When the panel is lifted, it should be kept as vertical as possible and washed with a jet of water so that the waste water will run into a basin, thereby collecting the washed-off sand for further use. When the panel is completely dry, any trimming or touching up can be done.

A variation in technique

If modelling on a flat clay surface is undertaken, and a wall (clay or wood) built around, plaster can be poured in, backed by plaster-soaked scrim or burlap, and allowed to set. By using a plastic sheet, it is possible to turn the whole panel over quite easily, and then the still moist clay can be removed. The modelling thus exposed will be in reverse, which often adds an unexpectedly interesting quality. (Plaster texture panel p. 26.)

It is, of course, necessary to carve or model in a flat manner, taking care to avoid overhangs which might make it difficult to remove the clay from the matrix.

Basic form mould

It is sometimes convenient to make a hollow shape which can be subsequently developed by manipulation and additions of clay.

1 Take a fist-sized lump of clay and, by slapping etc., shape it into a form which has smooth contours and which fits pleasantly into the hand. Use this as a basic shape. Allow it partly to dry so that its shape is not easily damaged.

2 Prepare a slab of clay somewhat thicker than the clay shape. Hollow out the middle to make a place for the shape. Carefully model the flat slab round the shape, so as to half bury it, seeing that there are no 'overhangs' to trap the plaster. Square off the edges of the slab and build a wall round as for a press-in mould.

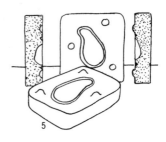

3, 4 Fill up the trough with plaster, and when it is set, turn it upside down so that the clay slab is now uppermost. Remove the clay wall and slab, so as to leave the 'master' shape in position in the plaster. Two or three holes or 'natches' should be made in the outer area (use a wire-ended tool or a teaspoon). Clean it up and build the clay wall again.

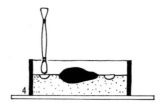

5 Brush thin ball clay slip over the whole plaster surface. Allow it to set a little, and then fill it up with fresh plaster. When it is hard, separate as for a press-in or mushroom mould. Finally, carve a channel about $\frac{1}{2}''$ wide x $\frac{1}{4}''$ deep, and about $\frac{1}{4}''$ from the lip of the shape.

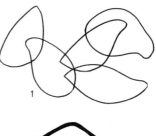

The clay will need to be rolled out fairly thin, since the form is not very big. Cut an area a little larger than the matrix, and coax it down into the hollow with the help of a moist sponge. When it is properly in, trim off the waste clay with a needle, leaving a little clay projecting above the edge. Do the same for the other half, and moisten the edges with slip and press them firmly together so that the 'natches' match up. Excess clay will spread into the groove.

If the mould is dry, it will be only a few minutes before the clay has shrunk sufficiently to allow the shape to be withdrawn.

Excess clay can now be trimmed ('fettled') off and the join made good. The shape can now be developed in any way that seems appropriate. For example, using the handle pulling technique, it can be elongated, or it may be pushed in, or protrusions may grow (for legs perhaps) from lumps of clay added, as for the feet on a dish. Pellets of clay, or flat, cut shapes, or ropes can be added, and so on. Particularly interesting work can be done with bird and animal shapes. It must be remembered that until you make a hole in it, you are really modelling round a bubble of air. This is very useful, as it gives the soft clay considerable strength. However, you *must* make a small hole before you finish.

Basic form birds: simple applied clay development. Made by adult.

6 Coiled pottery

There are many ways of making coiled pottery, all of which can be described in detail, but ultimately you will evolve your own technique. The important thing is to be able to make and use coils swiftly and with understanding. The style described here demands that each rope of clay is always added to the *inside edge* of the pot and subsequently stretched to the exact size required by finger pressure. This produces strong pottery and allows considerable control over shaping. The beginning, as in nearly all forms of pottery, is a ball of clay.

First stages

Base A ball of clay (orange size) is slapped into shape and placed on a bat. Using pressure from the heel of the hand it is flattened to make a really round disc, the edges and middle all being equal. Lift it carefully from the bat and ease the edges up all round to make a flattish saucer shape.

Coils Make ropes (see p. 30) the thickness of your thumb. They will be thinned down later. Discard any lumpy or not round. Roll them on the bench if necessary, but be sure to dampen it. When you are skilled you will not need to do this. Make several at a time and cover them with a moist cloth until you need them.

First coil Measure off slightly more rope than you need. Break it off by twisting with the fingertips. Place the rope on the *inside* edge of the saucer shape and allow to overlap about $\frac{1}{2}''$. Taper the overlapping ends, smear with slip, place together and smear joins over. Place ring in position and smear the inside on to the base. Do this quickly

and evenly. Now work round coaxing the outer and inner rings together, using finger and thumb. By gentle pressure the two thicknesses will be reduced to the size of one, and the pot opened a little. It is important to take care that there is no unequal nipping or pinching with its consequent unequal expansion. A good example will hardly show evidence of finger-marks anyway. Be quick and consistent.

All subsequent ropes are joined slightly differently... from now on it is the outside that receives attention first.
1 Fit rope to *inside* edge, taper and join edges, and place in position on inside edge.
2 In joining ropes, always smear from one to the other, just enough to make contact. Do this three or four times at intervals to tack the rope into position and then, fast and consistently, work round, smearing a little clay *upwards* with your thumb (fingers inside). Do not mess it about. Be very direct. Similarly (thumb inside, fingers over the opposite side) smear a little of the inside clay *downwards*.

So far there has been no *squeezing* at all.
3 Now the rope has been joined and the shape has to be considered. Use thumb inside and fingers outside (opposite side) and squeeze slightly as the pot is turned. This squeezing and turning assumes a rhythm. It should be light, rapid, and very consistent. In this way the

clay is stretched to assume the profile shape desired. The profile will move outwards (by squeezing), or upright (by less squeezing), or remain inwards (by not squeezing at all).

You aim to create good sound form that will require little
or no modification, and indeed good coiling will tend to produce satisfying forms simply because the material is handled
rightly. The pot itself will tend to take control and, sympa-
thetically followed, will usually produce a good shape. Often,
however, additional treatment is needed to control or modify
an existing shape, or to exploit some decorative possibility.
This usually involves the use of pressing or beating to move
the clay inwards or outwards according to the needs of the
moment.

Completing the shape

Your activity changes according
to the state of the clay. If it is
fairly soft and pliable, a good
deal can be done from the
inside, using a metal or kidney
presser and pressing outwards
and upwards against a hand
held on the outside of the pot.

Bulges may also be controlled
by using a presser from the
outside. It is wise always to
use the presser with an
upward movement and to keep
the pot rotating, so that the
work is consistent all round.

As the clay hardens a little,
a flat piece of wood used to
beat the pot gently can work
wonders, so long as you keep
the pot on the move. In the
early stages a misshapen pot,
turned upside down, can be
greatly improved.

The marks left by beating are
very decorative and should be
used with deliberation.

Small, bumpy surface
irregularities are best dealt with
by toothed scrapers which cut
across the bumps and expose
hollows which can then be
filled with pellets of clay and
rescraped. Constantly change
the direction of scraping to
avoid digging holes.

At intervals the flexible metal scraper is used to smooth off the toothed scraper marks. This scraper is only really effective if it is held in a state of tension, i.e. between the thumb and fingers so that it is slightly curved and nearly vertical to the clay surface. Used like this it will, firmly applied, shave off clay freely.

Tooth-edged and plain scrapers, used alternately, will quickly produce a smooth and controlled outline. The textural qualities of the toothed scraper should be observed and used to the full. The nature of the tool and its use in relation to the shape are valuable points of departure.

Further coiling ideas

Upside down coiling
Wide-mouthed pots with small bases are conveniently made from the upside down position. It is a good idea to start with a chalk circle and a large bat as a guide for the first few ropes. These are joined in the normal manner but encouraged to slope inwards as the pot grows (Fig. a). The final touch is a flattened ball of clay which becomes the base when the pot is inverted (Fig. b).

Developments If the first ropes are kept moist enough (moist cloths inside and out during later stages), building may be continued once the pot has been turned right way up (Fig. c).

Alternatively, two identical pots started at the same time

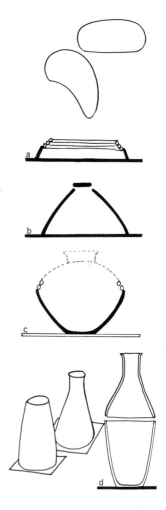

may be worked simultaneously and when strong enough, put together to make a large one (Fig. d).

Coiling has numerous uses and turns up in every phase of pottery.

'Upside down' coil pot, using rope and smearing as decoration. Made by adult.

Two 'upside down' shapes joined. Deeply carved surface oxided and glazed. Heavily grogged clay. Made by adult.

58   Coil pot shapes tend to be round by the nature of their manufacture, but will assume their own forms as they develop. This may be round, but is more likely to be asymmetrical, and none the worse for that. A ready recognition of what is good in form and an acceptance of the way the pot is developing itself are desirable. It must be recognised that the coil pot is not a substitute for a wheel-made pot, whose whole form expresses its mechanical origin, and its form will express its own way of manufacture.

If the coiling and making are well done, there will be a natural rhythm of coiling and smearing which itself is productive of incidental but interesting surfaces. The finger markings themselves or the ropes can be decoratively accentuated. Nothing, however, looks worse than badly made ropes and a misshapen form which has to be justified as 'interesting'. Good technique and an understanding of the form made are vital.

Clearly, although a well conceived and well carried out form is desirable, there is much scope for decorative treatment of the surface. One word of caution: do try to see that whatever you do arises from the nature of the pot itself, the nature of the materials used, and the nature of the techniques employed. It is unwise to start with an already established idea which is to be imposed on the pot. Do not let those magnificent museum pieces mislead you.

Final note: tall pots

A small kiln is not necessarily a limitation. Large pots can be made very satisfactorily if they are designed to be cut at suitable points. They can be fired separately (all to exactly the same temperature, so as to get the same degree of shrinkage) and subsequently stuck together again.

Adhesives like Bondcrete and Araldite (in Great Britain) and various epoxies in the United States are simple to use and very strong.

The pot should be cut when it has reached the leather hard stage. Cut earlier, it may get pushed out of shape, and later it will be too hard and may break.

'If the coiling is well done, there will be a natural rhythm of coiling and smearing which is productive of incidental and interesting surfaces.' Made by adult.

7 Slab pottery

Generally this means any work made in the first instance from flat sheets of clay and, more particularly, such items as panels, tiles, and boxlike forms. Although the rolling pin and canvas or burlap technique is the mainstay, there are other useful ways of making slab.

Cut slabs

Prepare a well-wedged lump of clay and make it into a squared shape by bumping it on the bench. Select two strips of wood of the thickness wanted for the tiles. Put one each side of the clay. Using them as a guide, drag a cutting wire through the clay. The wire must be held taut, with the thumbs firmly down on the guide strips. Lift off the top clay, place it down on the bench and begin again.

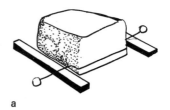

a

A more sophisticated method involves making a simple cutting frame from a length of iron rod (any springy metal will do). This is bent into a wide-open U shape and has notches cut at, perhaps, $\frac{1}{4}''$ intervals on the extremities. A cutting wire is stretched across tightly. The depth of cut is controlled by adjusting the level of the wire. Its use is shown in Fig. b.

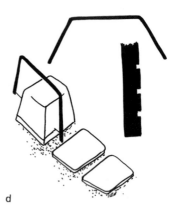

d

These are quick ways of making fairly small slabs (up to about 12"). Really large slabs can be undertaken quite easily, so long as proper preparations are made. It is wise to use heavily grogged clay (fireclay, sand or coarse grog), as this reduces the shrinkage and permits it to dry more evenly and quickly.

Large panels, limited only by the size of the bench, can be made and fired in a small kiln by simply cutting the slab up into convenient sections at the leather hard stage.

Large panels

1 On a bench or similar flat surface nail down the wooden strips ($\frac{3}{4}''$ x $1''$) so that their inner edges make the size of the proposed panel.

Dust the whole of the surface liberally with fine grog or flint powder to resist sticking clay and to provide a surface along which shrinking clay can move.

2 Take well grogged clay and begin to put down lumps at one end, filling the edges carefully. As the filling progresses, use a solid block of wood to beat the clay flat so as to consolidate it well within the framework. Also use a strip of wood to keep the clay level with the edge strips.

3 Build up the design in any suitable way (applied clay, carved, free modelling, stamps, slip, oxides etc.) then, when the clay has started to harden, cut the slab up into convenient sizes with due regard for the design.

4 As soon as possible remove the framework and carefully lift each section on to thin strips of wood so that the air can circulate beneath, and so as to allow drying from both sides.

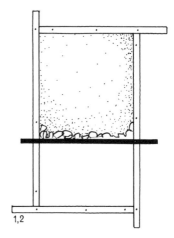

1,2

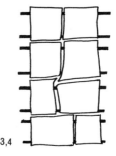

3,4

Large panel with applied decoration made by cutting up dish shapes. Made by adult.

Alternative panel method

Select a large board or flat surface and liberally sprinkle with flint or grog.

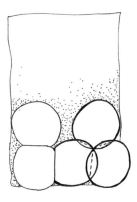

Roll out slabs of clay, using guide sticks so as to make them all the same thickness, just as for a dish. Place the first at one end of the prepared surface. Then put the next in position slightly overlapping the first. As each slab is put in position, use a needle to cut through both overlaps. Carefully avoid disturbing the main pieces as you take away the waste, and allow the main pieces to fit together.

As you can see below, the main panel has been made like this, and then children have each made separate bird shapes (with pressed and stamped decorations) which have been inserted in the same manner.

Mounting and hanging panels

Tile, ceramic and plaster panels are not really complete until some method of mounting, fixing and hanging is found.

The sandcasting method outlined on p. 49 is a useful way of combining smaller pieces of pottery or plaster into a panel, but this in itself needs mounting and hanging. If large and heavy pieces are to be fixed direct to a wall, the advice of a builder should be sought, but large panels, separately mounted and hung, are quite within the reach of the amateur.

Plaster can easily be drilled with an ordinary hand-drill and can effectively be bolted directly to a hardboard panel which has previously been framed and painted with emulsion paint. Washers should be used under the screw head, and the holes should be made a minimum of 1″ from the corners.

Larger, predominantly ceramic panels are heavier and require a different fixing. A simple and convenient base board can be made.

Prepare a piece of hardboard some inches larger than the ceramic panel. Back it solidly with 2″ x 1″ strips of wood, stuck with an impact glue (contact cement) and nailed. Use 'wriggle nails' for the accurately cut butt joints. Clean up outside edges carefully. Builder's merchants or hardware stores supply a very

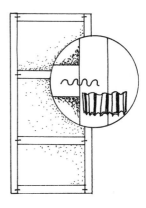

powerful adhesive (Bondcrete) which can be diluted with water, stained with powder paint and then mixed with sand. The background panel is first 'sized' with a diluted and coloured mixture (stone, concrete or dark colours are suitable backgrounds) and then, when all is dry, an undiluted mixture of sand and coloured adhesive is liberally applied to the whole surface and edges. The ceramic slabs have the back similarly covered, and are placed in position and left untouched for 24-48 hours. All that now remains is to fill the gaps between the slabs with 'grout', i.e. thin plaster or cement, or the prepared fire cement which one gets from a builder's merchant or hardware store.

Your panel may now be hung as for a framed picture.

Boxes and bottles

This is a very suitable technique for a wide range of boxes, bottles and constructions using the particular qualities of flat clay, cut as slabs or rolled. The chief problem is to persuade flat clay to dry flat.

It has already been noted that to make clay dry flat it is necessary to dry it equally from both sides, and that plaster slabs are useful in this respect. However, since clay must be constructed and joined in the leather hard stage, this is only part of the battle. Drying is helped by the use of a specially prepared mixture of grog or fireclay, but it is also very necessary to see that the clay dries very slowly (away from heat) so that all sides dry equally.

It is wise to prepare all the slabs for a particular piece of work at the same time, so that they start with the same degree of moisture and will therefore all shrink to the same extent. It is best to allow them to dry to the leather state, so that they have some strength and can be handled safely. Paper patterns can be cut as a rough guide, but they cannot really be used with any precision. A simple box, which would be the basis for a varied development, can be constructed as follows.

Cut the base slab to the exact inside measurement required. Cut the sides to the height needed, but leave an inch or two spare on the length. If they are assembled round the base in the manner indicated, they support themselves conveniently. Use some thick slip along the join, press the sides firmly together, wipe off the excess slip and then run a thin roll of clay along the inside of the join. Smooth it in neatly. Add all the sides and then cut off the excess clay, exposing the joins which must be very thoroughly completed.

This is best done by 'stitching' the join across with a modelling tool, so that clay is dragged across from one side to the other and finally smoothed off. These joins are more likely to come adrift than

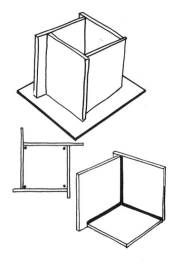

any other kind. Do them thoroughly. The base, in particular, is likely to be forgotten.

Slab pot with applied clay pressed decoration. Coiled neck, grey glaze. Made by adult.

Simple slab pot: incised decoration, oxided and scraped. Made by adult.

Pinched pot: shaped edge. Red clay dipped edgeways into glaze. Made by adult.

Pinch pot: two joined. Wax brushwork under copper oxide, blue glaze. Made by adult.

Triple pinch pot: manganese oxide (dry clay) under tin oxide. Made by child.

The squareness of the form can be reinforced by careful
beating and scraping. Although this is essentially a flat form
of work, avoid directly rectangular and square shapes with
dead straight lines. In the first place it is practically impos-
sible to get them, and in any case subtly curved lines are
much more satisfactory. Make a virtue of necessity.

It should also be borne in mind that many other ways of
using the slab can be found. It can be adapted to round
shapes, ovals and pots with more than four sides. Developments can also include using other techniques to make
taller, bottle-like shapes.

The full range of decorative techniques can be used, but
those involving pressed, stamped and applied clay are particularly suitable.

8 Pinch pottery

This is a deceptively simple way of making pottery. Make
no mistake about that. A well-made pinch pot is something
to be proud of. It will certainly test your capacity to respond
to the changing state of the clay. The forms are, in the main,
very simple and elegant and very characteristic of the way
they are made.

As always, begin with a lump of clay slapped into a round
shape (Fig. a). Hold it on the hand (a warm hand dries the
clay rapidly, so hold the hand open), and use the thumb from
the other on top with the fingers alongside (Fig. b). In this
position press and squeeze as you rotate the clay, working
the thumb ever deeper into the ball (Fig. c). Use absolutely
equal pressures in all directions, with frequent little move-
ments and pressures, leaving no large thumb or finger-
marks to be seen. Try to avoid opening the top, but concentrate on getting the thumb in as far as it will go. Make
the base as thin as you dare (Fig. d). Go right through if
necessary, to find out what it feels like. Cut samples up with
a wire to see. Once you have satisfied yourself that the base
is right, work upwards, spiralling as you go. Squeeze very
regularly.

From time to time you must pause to rest your hand, or wait for the clay to harden. Always put the pot down with the opening downwards (Fig. a), so as preserve its shape until the final stage, when stability may be given by hollowing out a little clay from the base to leave a ring on which the pot stands (Fig. b). The strength and grace of a pinch pot depends upon the arching shape and the tapering section which arises naturally out of good handling.

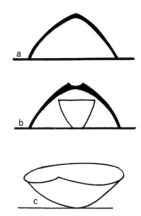

Simple adjustments to the edges, cut with a knife and sponged, will produce very delicate shapes (Fig. c).

Once you have gained control of the simple basic shapes, experiment with joined pots to increase your range. This is best done at the leather hard stage, but soft pots can be supported in a 'cradle' (Fig. d) until they are stronger. Joins must be carefully 'stitched' and smoothed over. Shapes can be controlled and improved by gently beating and scraping, and can be further developed by adding clay ropes.

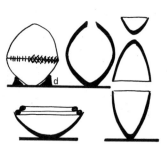

Decorative possibilities

While the full range of techniques may be used for pinch pottery, great restraint is desirable. The elegance of the form is the thing. This may be very satisfactorily burnished, particularly with red clays. Stamping and pressing, applied clay, wax resist and dipping in slip and glaze are all worth investigating.

Part dry shapes, cut up and reassembled, open up many interesting model and construction possibilities.

9 Potter's modelling

Potter's modelling may be defined as modelling whose character is determined by the application of specific pottery techniques. The essential thing is that not only should its construction involve a particular way of handling clay, but that this should show in the appearance. The range of possibility is limited only by one's capacity to handle techniques and material. The following suggestions indicate some lines to follow.

Squeezed clay
A large lump of clay is grasped firmly in both hands and squeezed vigorously. The result, looked at imaginatively, suggests further development. Although modified, it remains a piece of squeezed clay.

Rolled clay
Flat clay, nearly leather hard, is curved and cut and joined. The aim is to build a tall, self-supporting structure.

Slapped clay
A ball of clay is slapped into a comfortable 'hand' shape and then developed by gentle hand pressures and slappings.
Applied clay pellets are pressed home with a modelling tool.
The plain surface is burnished with a teaspoon. The inside is hollowed to remove air bubbles and to allow drying.

Pulled model, 4½" high. Dipped in brown glaze. Made by adult.

Pulled clay

This is the handle-making technique. The starting point is a ball of clay slapped into potato shape. Bumps are coaxed upwards by stroking (balls can be applied as for dish feet) to make embryonic legs, heads, tails etc. The figures are made separately and similarly, and added to the group later.

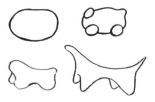

As the bumps are extended (use water and a stroking movement), they must taper outwards from the body. They will be very soft and weak, and unable to support the weight. A support must be made until the legs harden. Assemble it at the leather hard stage.

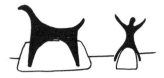

Rolled and folded

Suitably curved thin sheets of clay are endowed with considerable strength. Try working as follows:

1 Roll out thin, flat clay (use ¼″ wood strips).

2 Tear newspaper to the same size.

3 Fold paper in half and roughly tear the outline, side, view, of an animal (head, two legs, tail). Broad shapes are essential. Place on the clay.

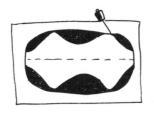

4 Cut round with a needle. Preserve the waste clay for further use.

5 Make a clay support about the same length as the paper pattern.

6 Drape the flat clay over the support and, using a finger as a mould, shape the legs round it. Coax, do not press.

7 Gradually increase the roundness in every direction. Strength comes from an unbroken round line. Finally lift away from the support.

8 Decorate with flat clay waste. Stamped pattern and texture can be made while it is flat.

Folded flat clay figures: animal shows the texture of the canvas. Figures stamped, folded, fired, glazed and scraped. Made by adult.

Hen and chicks: coiled pot.
Made by child.

Fish: joined dishes.
Made by adult.

Other modelling techniques

A little experimentation will quickly reveal other possibilities
with ropes of clay of varying thickness for animal and human
forms. Techniques which lend themselves to modelling, but
are not quite so obviously 'potter's' modelling, are shown
here.

The rope of clay loses its identity in the smoothed coil pot
and emerges differently. The pot form, pushed, beaten and
re-shaped, with clay applied, assumes a new character, although the pot remains.

It has already been suggested elsewhere that dishes lend
themselves to this. The fish example shown above began as
two joined dishes, with clay subsequently added. The others
are all basically coil pots.

Face: coiled pot, applied and
carved clay. Made by child.

Bird: coiled pot, oxided and
scraped. Made by adult.

10 Decorative techniques

Any interested person visiting museums and shops cannot
fail to realize the infinite range of pottery achievement - the
extraordinary sophistication of some and the magnificent
simplicity of others. An awareness of pottery achievement is
an excellent background, but it would be quite inappropriate to attempt to reproduce what was achieved in different times, under different circumstances, using very
different materials and with different social needs. There
ought to be an awareness of tradition and the ways of tradition, but no slavish following of it for its own sake. What
is attempted should reflect our own response to the materials and techniques we are using, and our understanding
of how they behave for us. In this sense we can approach
the best in pottery of all ages and cultures.

The beginner would do well to recognise the value of
limitations, of materials as well as techniques, and should
strive to work within them. If at all times we are concerned
about the nature of the materials and tools we employ - the
fluidity of slip, the quality of a soft brush stroke, the scrapi-
ness of a scraped mark, the beaten flatness and texture of
beaten clay, (the 'clayness' of clay in fact), and the right-
ness of form (a *beaten* shape, a *slab* shape, a *coiled* form)
- then it will probably end well. There must be a unity
between form and decoration, the materials and the tools.
It is important for the decoration to arise out of the work
in hand, not from the imposition of an external idea.

This sequence of decorative possibilities is controlled by
the changing nature of clay, but much of it can be applied
at every stage.

Decoration through making

Moist plastic clay: *fingers* The natural fingermarkings
arising from handling, smearing and joining can be subsequently emphasised with slip, oxide and glaze - and by
scraping the surface. The natural shape of coiling and fingering can be emphasised, unglazed, slipped, or glazed.

Leather hard clay (soft): *tool marks* The incidental marks
of making, scraping, smoothing with toothed scrapers can
be used. Also the marks of beating and the deliberate accen-
tuation of what started as incidental marks. Slips and oxides
can be used and scraped away, and glaze applied and
scraped.

Stamped marks These can arise from the making process. They can also be pressed by fingers or tools deliberately, or made by 'found' objects and specially made stamps and roulettes.

Applied clay The surface can be changed by adding clay in the form of pellets, coils and slabs. These may be stuck with thick slip or more securely 'thumbed' down decoratively. Stamps may also be used to secure the applied clay.

Carved clay This involves removal as opposed to addition. A heavy pot may be made more satisfactory by the thinning effect of carving, and an elegant one may catch light and shade attractively if the surface is broken by carved marks. Any implement, including the finger nail, may be pressed into service. Carved areas can be filled with thick slip or soft clay (of a similar nature, but different colour), and the surface scraped at a dryer stage to produce an inlay.

Leather hard clay (hard): *incised lines* With a harder surface, lines scratched or carved may be filled with oxide or slip (or glaze if fired first), and scraped off.

Sgraffito Alternatively the whole surface could be covered with slip or painted with oxide and, when dry enough, scratched so as to expose the under colour.

Burnishing Leather hard clay will produce a very high polish if it is rubbed with a smooth object, such as a tea-spoon, a toothbrush handle and so on. This is best on a brown or red clay. The polish becomes more definite as the clay hardens. This is particularly suitable for pinch pottery.

Slip and slip trailing

There is a whole category of pottery under the general name of slipware which is outside the scope of this book (see Further Reading), but it is necessary to deal with some aspects of slipware in detail. So long as it is remembered that slip is only used on moist clay, it can be applied by all the usual painting, pouring and dipping methods. There are some specialised techniques worth knowing about.

Trailing Slip trailers are normally of two types, the flat-tened balloon and the rubber bulb. The first is filled from a funnel and the second by expelling the air from the bulb before dipping it into the slip. A glass or plastic nozzle is then inserted. The consistency of the slip is important. It must be well sieved, and should be just thick enough to cling to a dipped finger in a creamy layer.

Stamped, oxided, scraped, fired, glazed, fired. Made by adult.

Applied clay, slip poured, scraped, fired, glazed, scraped, fired. Made by adult.

Coil pot: carved, oxided, scraped, fired, glazed, fired. Made by adult.

Incised, slip poured, scraped, fired, glazed, scraped, fired. Made by child.

Grey clay, wax resist, manganese oxide, fired, glazed, white glaze, fired. Made by child.

Grey clay, poured and trailed slip, transparent glaze. Made by adult.

Using the slip trailer Before you attempt any decoration, you will need to get the hang of it. Use an empty bench surface. Stand with feet apart, well balanced, so that the whole of your body may take part. These trailers perform quite differently. The bulb requires a positive squeezing movement, while the flattened balloon permits a free flow as soon as the nozzle tips downwards. Both will drip freely, especially if the slip is too thin. Experiment freely, with lines, scrolls, dots etc., but never actually touch the nozzle on the bench.

Feathering, marbling and fingering These are special techniques peculiar to the use of the slip trailer.

1 Prepare rolled out clay and transfer it to a board on which there is some newspaper (stops sticking and subsequent danger of cracking).

2 Strip the barbs off a feather to expose the springy tip (other similar ideas, such as a broom bristle, will do).

3 Fill a trailer with white (ball clay) slip.

4 Pour red slip on to the rolled out clay. Tilt to encourage it to run over all areas evenly.

5 While it is still wet begin to trail lines from side to side, closely and at graduated distances.

6 Drag the springy tip of the feather lightly across the surface at right angles to the lines of white slip, so dragging dark slip across white. Drag in the reverse direction too. Try variations. Employ several colours, using circles, spots and various combinations.

ien you have a successful attern, bump the board gently to spread the slip. Allow it to dry to a touchable state, then use on a mushroom mould. (See pp. 42-3.) If it is no good, try marbling. By using the feather freely in any direction or by lifting the board and using a jerking, swirling, tipping movement, encourage the slip to make 'movement' patterns or allow all the free slip to run off in one controlled direction and so on. If it is still unsatisfactory, wipe all the slip off with a kidney presser and start again. This may be done several times.

7 Fingering is very direct.

Use dark clay with white slip poured over it. Drain it off well and bump it a little to settle it down. Then make combed patterns by lightly moving the fingers across the surface, so exposing the dark clay below. This is a very traditional idea.

These ideas have applications in any kind of decoration, but particularly for press-in and mushroom moulds. Note especially that the slip must be touchable dry for use with a **press-in mould, and that the** clay should be put into the **mushroom moulds before** decoration starts. The difference in moulds will produce very different results.

Simple slip trailing: brown slip with white trailed over. Made by adult.

For use on moist, leather hard, dry, biscuit, underglaze and onglaze (overglaze) All metals produce oxides, only some of which have practical applications so far as ceramics are concerned. Prepared versions (underglaze colour, body and glaze strains etc.) are available. They are more expensive than straight oxides and are not necessarily more useful in this context. A very limited range of oxides is needed really.

Some oxides tend to disappear at higher temperatures, others are too expensive or only produce their best colours under special conditions. This means that the range of useful colours is fairly limited anyway. In practice it is difficult to produce adequate reds, but blues, greens, browns, yellows, white and black are possible, and these are very varied according to the way in which they are used. The type of clay, the type of glaze, the temperature etc. all affect the end product. You cannot see directly (as with paint) what the final colour will be.

Mixing and use of oxide For most normal purposes it is quite sufficient to mix with water to a milky consistency and apply directly with a brush. Rather more consistent colour can be made by grinding the colour on a tile with a palette knife, though it is hardly needed in this context. Keep your oxides in separate labelled pots. They all tend to look alike - black - since their true colour does not emerge until after firing. Oxides may be intermixed, but keep records of what you do - you may want to repeat it. The amount of oxide that you apply matters, and it is not simple to control. Circumstances affect the result very much. For example on moist clay, which will not absorb water, the result is thin. On a biscuit pot, however, the story is different as the water is readily soaked up, leaving an excessive layer of oxide on the surface. Getting a good balance of oxide is important, as too much will result in metallic blacks (good if you happen to want them), too little will fade or disappear. The right amount will produce good colour. Other factors must also be borne in mind. Too slow a brush stroke will allow too much water to soak into the pot, and leave behind too much oxide. The oxide, being heavy, settles to the bottom of the mixture rapidly, so keep it stirred everytime you dip.

Don't be put off by all the warnings!

Oxide may be used in almost every context and with practically every technique of painting, scraping and resisting, and also as a colourant for slips and glazes.

Oxides suitable for general use:

Cobalt carbonate Blue. Very powerful colorant. Rarely good alone, but used in very small amounts mixed with another oxide is excellent.

Copper carbonate Green. Looks green in powder form. Black if used in excess. Produces various greens according to use with alkaline or lead glaze. Good with tin in the glaze.

Manganese oxide Purplish browns to black. Looks black in powder form. Mixes well with other oxides. Must not be used in excess. Tends to melt at biscuit temperatures and there is a danger of pots sticking together. Be careful when firing dry clay.

Iron oxide (Ferric oxide, black iron oxide, scarlet iron oxide) Variations on a theme. Colours range from yellows to reddish browns.

Chrome oxide A nasty hard green unless used in very tiny amounts. Tin glazes tend to show pink in its presence. Needs using with caution.

Note All oxides need to be kept under strict control. Minute particles can spoil otherwise clear glazes. So can thumb-prints transferring oxide from point to point.

Resists

The resist technique involves any means whereby slip, oxides or glaze are prevented from touching the surface of the pot. It is used at any stage in manufacture. There are three principal methods used.

Wax resist Normally it is necessary to heat the wax. This means using a double saucepan of some kind to prevent the danger of burning. A small glue pot is excellent. Ordinary candle wax, together with about one third thin machine oil or paraffin (kerosene) makes a good mixture which should be well heated. The wax is painted on and the resulting mark is much modified by the kind of brush used. Try using bristle as well as soft hair brushes. Since the wax hardens swiftly, a decisive use of the brush is desirable. Do not stand with the brush poised while you think.

Wax crayons, plain or coloured, are also used with rather different qualities.

Once the wax is applied, slip, oxides or glaze are brushed or poured over, or the pot is dipped. They adhere only to the unwaxed portion. The wax burns off during firing. It may smell somewhat, so be warned. It is not suitable for use on a moist surface.

Paper resists Thin paper - tissue, Japanese rice paper or similar - may be torn or cut and stuck down on to a moist surface (clay or slip is best). Slip (engobe) or oxide are then painted or poured over and left to dry to the touchable state. The resist is then peeled off for new resist work or final drying. It is worth noting the special qualities of torn shapes as opposed to cut shapes.

Pink resist Special preparations can be obtained from manufacturers which, mixed with water, may be painted direct on to the pottery to resist oxides, slip (engobe) or glaze. After firing, the surface colour may be wiped off to expose the under layers.

It is quite possible to use the differing qualities of these resists on the same piece of work.

11 Glaze

What it is
Almost every aspect of pottery is essentially simple but capable of infinite complexity. Glaze is no exception. Essentially glaze is a glass-like material which is applied to the pottery as raw ingredients in carefully balanced proportions which are subsequently melted at specific temperatures and allowed to cool. The resulting material may be infinitely varied, according to the type and proportion of ingredient used, the amount of heat to which it is submitted and the kind of atmosphere in the kiln.

Its purpose may be defined as utilitarian and·decorative. In the first place it provides a means of making pottery able to contain fluids, and makes washing easy. In the case of food vessels, this is of first importance. Its decorative aspects are numerous and for us by far the most important.

The complexities of the subject need not concern the novice, since within a very limited range of glaze lies a great range of possibility. The basic needs are a transparent shining glaze and a transparent matt glaze. From these, with suitable modification and experiment, practically all normal needs can be met. If you want to explore the subject more fully, please see Further Reading list.

Although it is quite possible to make 'slip' glazes for use with unfired clay, it is convenient and usual to 'biscuit' pottery before glazing it. For a glaze to be technically satisfactory, it must 'fit' the pot. That is to say, its shrinkage and expansion rates must approximate to those of the pot itself.

For this reason, it is clear that not every glaze will do. If the pot shrinks more than the glaze, 'shivering' or peeling off takes place. Conversely, if it shrinks more than the pot, 'crazing' or cracking of the glaze takes place.

For a glaze to fit properly, it must be mixed to suit a particular clay and fired at a specific temperature to ensure a proper melting of the ingredients. Fortunately most manufacturers supply a line of glazes specially prepared for the clays they sell and will give information regarding firing temperatures. There is a bewildering range to choose from, but one's needs are simple. It is more expensive to buy prepared glaze, and the raw ingredients can be obtained just as readily. Glazes may, for our purposes, be divided into those containing soluble lead, those containing insoluble lead and those which are lead free. Lead is poisonous, and those glazes containing soluble lead are definitely dangerous for the novice to use. Those containing insoluble lead, as well as the lead-free, are safe. These are known as 'Fritt' glazes, which means that a proportion of the ingredients has been heated to melting point, cooled and powdered before being combined with the rest of the ingredients. Generally speaking, the lead Fritt glazes have a greater range of tolerance than the non-lead Fritt glazes, and are to be preferred. The average earthenware glaze has a melting point of about 1020° to 1120° C, and this suits most normal clays. Since you may be using a number of differing glazes on the same pot at the same time, it is as well to see that they are all compatible types. But it should be pointed out that the oddities arising from incompatible glazes (different melting points, for example), running, bubbling and so on, are often interesting and worth using deliberately.

How to prepare it
Glaze as supplied by the manufacturer requires little preparation other than mixing with water and passing through a 120 mesh sieve.

Glaze recipes can be expressed in a number of ways, and it is not easy to make comparisons between different recipes. They may be expressed as formulae, as percentage compositions or as parts by weight. The latter is a very practical way. As some recipes call for very small quantities, a fairly accurate set of scales is desirable.

The procedure is quite simple. Weigh all the ingredients dry and tip them in separate piles into the mixing bowl. Count them and compare with the recipe. It is surprising how easy it is to omit one ingredient when all are white and not easily distinguishable.

Mix them dry (the nylon household sink brush is excellent for this), and then stir in water until a heavy creamy mix is obtained. Leave it for some hours if you can, while it 'slakes' or soaks, then pass it through a sieve (60 mesh first and then 120). This can be conveniently arranged as follows.

Sticks or a wire cake tray are placed over a basin with the 60 mesh sieve in position (see Fig. b). Glaze mix is then ladled or poured into the sieve (use the half ball). Assisted by water (rubber pipe from the tap) and the nylon brush, pass it through. Lumps are flattened with the kidney presser.

Wash the 60 mesh sieve, brush, presser etc. in the bowl from which the glaze came (Fig. a), using as little water as possible so as not to waste any glaze, and pass the washing water through the 120 sieve (Fig. c) into the second bowl. Glaze is expensive. It is also necessary to pass all the ingredients through the sieve, lest you end up with an incorrect mix. Pass the main mixture through the 120 sieve and again wash up, once more passing all the washing water through the sieve so that everything ends up in the bowl. The glaze ought to pass through the sieve two or three times. Leave it to settle and then pour off the excess water, leaving a thin creamy mixture. Glazes may be stored indefinitely in a container with a lid, but will need stirring from time to time and must occasionally be resieved.

Base glaze recipes which can be developed

Shining transparent		Matt transparent	
Lead bisilicate	64.2	Lead sesquisilicate	52.6
China clay	21.0	Felspar	31.2
Cornish (or Cornwall)		China clay	7.2
stone	9.5	Whiting	5.6

Moulded dish: 'pulled' feet. Wax and oxide under grey glaze. Made by adult.

Moulded dish: dry clay, manganese oxide scraped off, then fired. Copper carbonate brushwork. Glazed with tin oxide. Made by child.

Edge to edge pinch pots: beaten, oxided, scraped, fired, glazed and scraped again. Made by adult.

Pinch pot: shape beaten and carved, thin white glaze. Made by adult.

Whiting	5.3	Flint (silica)	3.4	81
	100.0%		100.0%	

Both of these are expressed as percentages, but they may safely be weighed out in ounce or gram units. They both fire at 1050° to 1100° C and may be applied on each other.

Extending the range of base glazes
These glazes can be adjusted to produce an interesting range of texture and colour.

Stained glazes The transparent glaze is given colour by the addition of small quantities of oxide or glaze stain. They will still reveal what is under them but of course will change the colour. It, in turn, will be modified by what is under it.

Opaque glazes The transparent glaze (coloured or not) is rendered opaque by the addition of an opacifier (usually tin oxide). This means that the uncoloured transparent glaze is made white and will obscure what is under it. This in turn can have oxides added. It is usual to add about 10% tin oxide, but this can be varied. For example, a 5% addition used over a very red clay would allow the redness to break through attractively on a pot whose surface was textured.

Double glazes and combined glazes There is a wide range or possibility in overglazing. If, for example, a pot is glazed with a matt white and immediately re-glazed with a shining olive green, as they melt together there will be a combining of the two. If there had been wax painted on the matt white before the second glaze was applied, this would have remained white surrounded by coloured glaze. Further, if, while the glaze was still unfired, areas had been scraped off to expose the natural unglazed surface as well, there would have been an interesting juxtaposition of glazed and non-glazed surfaces.

A totally different quality is imparted if the first glaze is fired before the second is applied. *Note:* the second glaze must be much thicker and the pot warmed before application, to allow for the non-absorbent state of the pot. In this state the first glaze permits of an interesting sgraffito technique, as the second glaze is scratched before re-firing.

Glazes, in their liquid state, may be mixed in definite proportions (so many cupfuls of each), but do keep exact records.

It must always be remembered that the nature of the pot will have a profound effect on the glaze. The nature of the oxides and slips under the glaze, as well as the clay of the pot and the thickness of the glaze mixture, all play a significant part.

Some simple glaze additions
You can extend the range of colour by the addition of simple oxides. One word of warning, however. Keep careful records of any experiments you make. Use your transparent shining and matt glazes as the base, and go on from there. It is not possible to predict the colours with exactitude, as they will be greatly influenced by the type of glaze in use.

White	5-10% tin oxide
Black	3% cobalt carbonate
	2% ferric oxide (iron oxide) } or 10%
	2% manganese oxide } manganese
Blue	½% cobalt carbonate
Green	2% copper carbonate
Light Brown	2% iron oxide
Brown	4% iron oxide
Grey	2% iron chromate

You should also try limited combinations of oxides, for example:

Grey/Blue	½% cobalt carbonate
	2% iron oxide
Purple/Blue	½% cobalt carbonate
	5% manganese oxide

How glaze is applied
Pottery is usually 'biscuited', or bisqued, before glazing is attempted. Since the biscuit, or bisque, fire is normally restricted to about 950-1000° C, the resulting pottery is porous and will readily absorb water. This makes glazing fairly simple, because as the water is soaked into the pot, so a layer of glaze is deposited on the surface. So long as it is remembered that the results vary according to the way the glaze is applied, then almost any means is acceptable. Every piece glazed is a special case and must be considered on its merits, and the means used will vary according to the shape, size, whether there is enough glaze and so on.

The usual ways are:

Dipping (Fig. a) If there is enough glaze, a deep enough container and an even layer is required, this is the most satisfactory way. The piece is grasped by a convenient part of the base in one hand, and if necessary supported with a finger from the other. The whole (hand and all) is dipped for a moment, withdrawn and shaken slightly to get rid of excess drips. As it is placed on a bat, the point of contact between finger and pot is covered with glaze running off the finger. This all needs a certain dexterity and planning.

Pouring (Fig. b) When there is a shortage of glaze, or the piece is not convenient for dipping, the glaze is poured into a jug or cup, the piece held over a basin and the glaze poured freely over all. It is also

usual in some cases to put the wire cake tray (or sticks) across the basin to support the piece while glaze is poured over.

Whatever glazing is attempted, it is necessary to consider well just how it is to be done. Rehearse each pot and decide just how and where you are going to put it down safely. In the case of flat dishes it is useful to make a series of 'claws' of varying sizes to help hold them without leaving fingermarks behind (Fig. c).

Painting is employed in cases where tne above methods are inappropriate. A soft brush is used to blob the glaze on.

Trailing, as in slip trailing, can also be effectively used to apply glaze over glaze.

Glaze is also sometimes sprayed, but this is not recommended unless a special exhaust fan has been installed, as the atomised glaze dust is injurious.

Final advice: Plan this carefully. Rehearse your moves. Do it without hesitations. The slower you are, the thicker the glaze. Really clean both the sink and yourself afterwards. Pottery dust can be injurious to health.

This section must inevitably repeat much of what has already been described earlier, but nevertheless glazes are by their very nature decorative and have their particular contribution to make. The use of glazes is not only a final stage (which it is for a good deal of work), but also a point of new departure. Apart from their basic use as a means of rendering the pot watertight and easily washed, they are employed in a number of definite ways.

1. *Already decorated ware* In cases where decoration is already complete (for example, a slip decorated dish, or a wax resist and oxide decoration), the function of the glaze is to reveal and emphasise. Use transparent shining or matt glazes with slip and opaque glazes over oxides (which will make their presence felt and will be modified by the glaze). See p. 73, bottom left.

2. *Glaze for its own sake* Where the pot has a plain, simple and complete form, self-coloured glaze, transparent, shining, matt or opaque may be effectively used purely for the quality of the glaze alone. Into this category would come textured and applied clay decoration, but the emphasis would be on the glaze. Glaze over a glaze of a different kind, and glaze applied over itself by careful dipping, so as to produce controlled areas of double glaze, should also be considered. (Facing p. 65, bottom).

3. *To augment and develop design* Under this heading comes the full range or possibilities. The aim is to extend the possibilities of slip and oxide and their associated techniques. Explore the qualities of glaze itself. Use it thick, use it thin. Try the juxtaposition of glazed and non-glazed surfaces. To this end use wax resist (permits no glaze at all), or scrape off areas (leaves some residual glaze), or rub glaze off to expose selected shapes. As opposed to the removal of glaze, try the addition of glaze. Use a brush to apply local areas to emphasise an otherwise unglazed surface. Double dip and double pour (as in 2 above) and use a slip trailer too. Use wax resist on glaze (or pink resist) and reglaze or paint with dilute oxide. Try using a shining glaze over a matt one and so on.

However much you become involved in acquiring experimental experience, and however interesting the results may seem, don't lose sight of the main aim, which is to produce a harmony between form, colour and surface. Keep firmly in mind the need for decoration to arise from the nature of the pot, the materials used and the tools to hand.

12 Kilns: packing and firing

Kilns are designed according to the type of fuel available, the volume of work to be fired and the maximum temperatures required. For most people this limits the choice of fuel to gas (town, natural or propane) or electricity, though coke, wood, coal or any other fuel could be used.

Gas and electric kilns have received much attention from manufacturers and many varieties are now available for the amateur. They range in size from little ones capable of running direct from the normal household supply to very large ones requiring installation by a kiln engineer. Two main types are in use: those opening from the top (see below) and those opening from the front. Sizes usually refer to the internal measurements, and they are quoted as being for specific maximum temperatures, 1100° C for earthenware and 1300° C for stoneware. To attempt to fire the lower temperature kiln to a higher temperature would result in damage to the kiln itself as well as burning out the elements. The stoneware kiln, of course, can be used to fire at the lower temperatures. It must be pointed out that the claims of electric kilns to fire at such high temperatures should be treated with reserve. It is done, but at the cost of a shorter element life. More expensive electrical types are being developed to overcome this limitation.

Whatever type you choose, the basic principles are the same - a slow increase of heat until the desired temperature is attained, followed by an equally slow and steady loss of heat until the pots may be removed at 'hand' heat.

Temperature indication

The temperature reached or, more accurately, the heat work done, is of first importance. The oldtime potter learned to judge this with surprising accuracy, using the colour of the pots as his indicator, backed up by tests withdrawn from the kiln at intervals.

The present-day potter may use either pyrometric cones, generally known as Seger cones, or an electrical device called a pyrometer.

The Seger cone is made from an accurately calculated glaze mixture which will soften at predetermined temperatures, thus giving a visual indication of the heat work done. The cones are best used in a sequence of three, chosen to bracket the desired temperature. For example, to indicate 1040° C, one cone to show 1020° C and one to show 1060° C would also be selected. They should be placed in a row, in a socket designed for the purpose, opposite the spy hole in the door, but some 6″-8″ in to avoid cold draughts. The temperature is correctly indicated if:-

No. 1 bends right down as a warning that the critical temperature is approaching.

No. 2 then bends over so that its tip is level with its base.

No. 3 remains upright as witness that the required temperature has not been exceeded.

The cones are placed in a slanting position so that they may bend properly when the time comes. No cone can be used twice. The temperature capability of each cone is shown by a code number stamped on each cone.

Front loading electric kiln of medium size.

The pyrometer is efficient, convenient and expensive. A thermocouple is inserted into the kiln and indicates continuously the changing temperature on a sensitive dial mounted on a nearby wall.

Temperature control

Electrical control devices are normal on all the larger kilns, and the rate of heating is adjusted simply by turning the dials to the appropriate numbers. Some smaller kilns may, however, need to be repeatedly switched on and off to restrict the rising temperature sufficiently during the early stages. With gas kilns it is a simple matter of turning the

taps (valves). The problem is to keep the temperature rising - but very slowly - hence the value of a pyrometer.

Kiln furniture

Ceramic shelves and shelf supports are necessary to allow even and economic packing of the kiln. It is important to get shelves etc. made of the right material for your particular kiln. A low firing kiln does not require such durable shelves as a high firing kiln, and it is no economy to buy cheap shelves and find that they have sagged because they cannot stand the heat. The supports must also be able to withstand the required temperatures. In Great Britain they are of three main types, pillar, domed and recessed, and castellated, and are designed to be stacked one on the other so as to build up any height required. Most American potters buy bricks of various shapes and sizes. It is essential to see that supports are placed exactly over each other so as to transmit the weight directly downwards. Supports arranged in triangular fashion are more stable than one at each corner of each shelf.

Gas kiln: Saviac kiln, maximum temperature 1300° C.

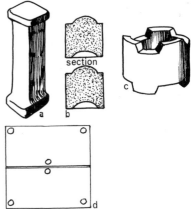

Stilts, spurs, saddles, etc.

There is a wide range of ceramic pieces whose job is to prevent glazed pottery from touching the kiln shelf and so sticking. They are available in many sizes, but on the whole there is no very great need for them if simple precautions are taken. First, the shelves should be well painted with a mixture of powdered flint (silica) and water every time the kiln is used. Second, the base of the pot must be well scraped and sponged to remove all glaze. Third, the glaze must be removed sufficiently far up the pot to allow for the possibility that the glaze may flow downwards. Fourth, care must be taken to avoid dropping bits of glaze on to the shelf.

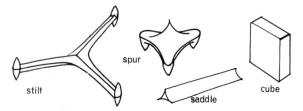

These are possibly the most useful types of placing furniture and can be made to serve most purposes.

Packing and firing
Successful firing depends upon a number of factors.
1 The clay must be very dry, free from air pockets and well constructed.
2 Pottery must be properly and safely placed in the kiln.
3 The rise in temperature must (for the first 500° C) be very slow indeed (to allow for complete drying and expansion).
4 There must be no sudden draughts (such as caused by opening the kiln door).
5 The necessary temperature must be reached.
6 Cooling must be as slow as the heating.
7 Patience, lest you open the kiln door too soon and cause 'dunting' (cracking due to sudden contraction).

Pottery is only complete when it has been 'fired' or 'burned', and this usually takes place in two stages, 'biscuit' and 'gloss'. This is only a matter of convenience, as it is quite possible to do both stages at the same time. 'Biscuit' is fired at around 1000° C, glazed and refired at temperatures between 1050° C (earthenware) to 1250° C (stoneware). Red or brown clays usually produce earthenware, and would melt at higher temperatures, while buff firing (grey clays) will make both earthenware and stoneware according to the temperature reached. It is, however, usual to have special mixes for stoneware.

The chief difference between packing for a 'biscuit' and a 'gloss' is that in a biscuit kiln the pieces may be allowed to touch each other, or even placed one on the other (so long as due consideration is given to the strength of each piece). Biscuit with oxide must be watched carefully as some oxides (notably manganese) melt a little at 1000° C and can cause sticking. For a 'gloss' it is essential that the pieces are placed away from each other (not closer than ¼") and the bases must be scrupulously cleaned, or put on to 'stilts'. The shelves must be washed with a flint wash.

Efficient packing calls for considerable patience and ingenuity. A kiln fires best when it is fully loaded, as there is a more even distribution of heat. A good deal of sorting out of pieces to decide where they should best be placed is necessary. Particularly with a biscuit (bisque), it must be remembered that dry clay can be very fragile. Many a good piece has been broken as it is placed in the kiln. Arrange the temperature cones so that they can be seen through the spy hole. Don't guess - try it out.

Use a torch, or flashlight, if necessary. You can be sure only when the door is shut. It is wise to consider leaving a little space between the shelves and the sides of the kiln to allow circulation of heat.

Firing routine

The 'switch on' can be as slow as you like, until there is no sign of moisture around the top spy hole. When this dries, advance the heat a little. When the blackness of the pottery begins to change to red heat, you may speed up a good deal. Do not be misled by the false glow of the elements. For biscuit (bisque), a maximum of 950-1000° C in 8 to 10 hours is quite fast enough. Faster, and you will have explosions amongst your pots. When the second cone bends, switch off, and allow it to cool for at least as long as it took to heat up.

A gloss (glaze) firing is much the same, except that the packing has to be very carefully done, and the preliminary heating up may go a little faster. When red begins to show, you may increase the heat up to about ¾ for some hours, and finally for the last few hours, to full pressure. The actual final temperature is determined by the kind of glaze used. A firing up to 1100° C· in 12 hours would be about right.

Please note: shelves should only be washed with flint (silica) on the top sides, lest pieces fall off on to glazed pottery. When the second cone has properly bent, switch off, put in the spyhole plugs and allow to cool. Don't be tempted to try to remove pieces too soon, or you will only ruin your hard work.

The kiln illustrated alongside was seen at Vallauris (Alpes Maritimes, France). It was built to fire a single tall pot and used wood for its fire.

If you live in an open area, you might well consider building a simple kiln for yourself. Much interesting work can be done if it is remembered that the essentials are very slow heating over a long period, followed by equally slow cooling. In kilns of this type, glaze is a dubious proposition, but work having stamped, pressed, applied clay and polished surfaces is worthwhile. Plans for an efficient coke-burning kiln are available (see List of Suppliers).

For further reading

A Potter's Book by Bernard Leach. Faber & Faber, London.
English Slipware by Dorothy Kemp. Faber & Faber, London.
Clay and Glazes for the Potter by Daniel Rhodes. Pitman, London. Chilton, Philadelphia.
Practical Pottery and Ceramics by Kenneth Clark. Studio Vista, London. Viking, New York.
The Technique of Pottery by Dora M. Billington. Batsford, London. Hearthside, New York.

List of materials

Clay: plastic (moist): grey (buff or white firing)
red or brown (red firing)
    powdered: grey
red or brown
ball clay (white burning for slip)
Grog: fine or medium
Sand: silver sand or washed freshwater sand
Plaster: slow setting potter's plaster
Oxides: red iron
    manganese (black or dioxide)
    copper (black or red) or copper carbonate
    cobalt (black waterground) or cobalt carbonate
    tin oxide
Slips (Engobes): a variety of coloured slips made from natural
    clays, or clays stained with oxides
Wax: paraffin wax (diluted with thin machine oil or paraffin, called
    kerosene in U.S.A.)
Glaze: to make your own base glaze, you need:
    lead sesquisilicate or lead bisilicate
    felspar
    china clay
    Cornish stone (Cornwall stone)
    whiting
    flint (silica)
    alternatively to buy ready made:
    transparent matt glaze (1050°-1100° C)
    transparent shining glaze (1050°-1100° C)
  This is in no way intended to be a full list, but just an indication
of basic needs. There is scope for considerable development
within the limitations of this range.

List of apparatus

Kiln: shelves, supports, Seger cones or pyrometer and various
    placing pieces (stilts, spurs, etc.).
Bench: a solid work surface.
Turntable: you can do without it, but it is very useful.
Bats: in quantity, any size or shape.
Storage: damp: for unused plastic clay, work in progress and clay
    being regenerated.

dry: for all the various powder mixtures, as well as shelf space for completed work.

Containers: as wide a collection of bowls, basins, buckets, cannisters (with lids) and jugs as you can manage. Preferably made of plastic.

Sieves: 8-10" in wooden frames, 60 and 120 mesh.

Brushes: artists: soft and hard, large and small.

housepainters: 1" and 2" are useful.

nylon: household sink brushes.

Slip trailers and nozzles

Cloths: for rolling out clay: canvas or hessian (burlap), at least 24" square.

floorcloths (rags): heavy duty.

Sponges: household cellulose sponges: heavy duty.

small 2-3" close texture natural sponges.

Rolling pin: 14-16", plain, no handles.

Wood strips: in matched pairs, 24" $\times$ $\frac{3}{4}$" or $\frac{1}{2}$"

pieces of wood to beat and shape clay.

Knives: any thin, short, narrow blade.

artist's palette knife (small, 6").

Cutting wires: nylon line (40 lb. breaking strain in U.K., 40 lb. test in U.S.A.) or 3 to 4 strands of thin copper wire tightly twisted.

Scrapers: home made from hacksaw blades, adhesive spreaders or bits of rasp plane blades.

flexible metal scrapers, kidney shaped as well as straight-sided, 3-4" long.

housepainter's scraper.

Pressers or ribs: kidney shaped, rubber with tapered off edges.

Modelling tools: of any kind, particularly simple wooden ones and large simple wire loops which have been given teeth by filing.

Needle pricker or pin: an adjusted hat pin is by far the best.

Wax pot: must have a water jacket (double boiler), otherwise danger of fire.

Wire cake tray: very useful in glazing, or where you want to dry from both sides.

Funnels: for filling slip trailers, pouring glaze into narrow pots. Those with a built in sieve are very useful for slip.

List of suppliers

Clay: Potclays Ltd., Copeland St., Stoke-on-Trent
  Podmore and Sons, Caledonian Mills, Shelton, Stoke-on-Trent
  United Clay Mines Corp., 101 Oakland St., Trenton 6, N.J.,
  U.S.A.
  Stewart Clay Co., 133 Mulberry St., New York, N.Y. 10013,
  U.S.A. Jack D. Wolfe Clay Co., Fry Meeker Avenue, Brooklyn,
  N.Y. 11222, U.S.A.
Glaze materials and oxides:
  Podmore and Sons (see above)
  Wengers Ltd., Etruria, Stoke-on-Trent
  American Art Clay Co., 4717 West 16th St., Indianapolis 24,
  Ind., U.S.A.
  Stewart Clay Co. (see above)
  Jack D. Wolfe Clay Co. (see above)
Plaster: Cafferata Ltd., Newark-on-Trent
  Bellman, Ivey and Carter, 110a Mill Lane, West Hampstead,
  N.W.6.
  United States Gypsum Co., 300 West Adams St., Chicago 6,
  Illinois, U.S.A. (for large quantities)
  Hardware or building supply stores for small quantities in
  U.S.A.
Sieves, scrapers, pressers and tools:
  Wengers Ltd. (see above)
  Stewart Clay Co. (see above)
Turntable, scrim, modelling tools:
  London Art Bookshop, 72 Charlotte St., London, W.1.
  Stewart Clay Co. (see above)
Kilns: Electric: Bernard Webber Ltd., Webcot Works, Alfred St.,
  Fenton, Stoke-on-Trent, Staffs.
  Cromartie Kilns Ltd., Dividy Rd., Longton, Stoke-on-Trent
  R. M. Catterson Smith Ltd., Adams Bridge Works, South Way,
  Exhibition Grounds, Wembley, Middx.
  British Ceramic Service Co. Ltd., Bricesco House, 1 Park
  Avenue, Wolstanton, Newcastle, Staffs.
  Norman Ceramics Co., 225 Namaroneck Avenue, Namaroneck,
  N.Y. 10544, U.S.A.
  Gas: Gibbons Bros. Ltd., Dibdale, Dudley, Worcs.
  Bernard E. Webber Ltd. (see above)
  A. D. Alpine, Inc., 11837 Teale St., Culver City, California,
  U.S.A.

Plans for coke kiln: Rosemary and Denise Wren, Potter's Croft, Oakshade Rd., Oxshott, Surrey

Plans for all types of kilns: American Craftsmen's Council, 44 West 53rd St., New York, N.Y. 10019, U.S.A.

Kiln furniture:

Acme Marls, Clough St., Hanley, Stoke-on-Trent

Acknowledgments

Photographs by Kenneth Drake. The author and publishers wish to thank the following for photographs and permission to reproduce them. (References are to page numbers.)

British Ceramic Service Co. 85

R. M. Catterson-Smith Ltd. 86

Bernard E. Webber (S-o-T) Ltd. 87

Index